The Complete Patter

Michael Munro
Illustrated by John Byrne

CANONGATE BOOKS

First published in Great Britain in 1996 by
Canongate Books Ltd
14 High Street
Edinburgh EH1 1TE

Reprinted 1998

Copyright © Michael Munro, 1996
Illustrations copyright © John Byrne 1988

British Library Cataloguing in Publication Data

A catalogue record for this volume is available
on request.

ISBN 0 86241 619 1

Typeset by Palimpsest Book Production Limited,
Polmont, Stirlingshire
Printed and bound by
WSOY, Porvoo, Finland

Introduction

In *The Patter* (Glasgow District Libraries, 1985) my intention was to record in print an impression of the dialect of Scots spoken in and around the city of Glasgow. At that time Glasgow's fortunes and self-image were on the rise, and the staging of the Garden Festival in 1988 and the year as European City of Culture in 1990 were both expressions and reinforcements of that improvement. Perhaps my book tapped into this spirit; in any case it seemed to strike a chord with Glaswegians at home and outwith the city, achieving sales to date of over 140,000 copies.

The Patter made its way all over the world, to wherever exiled Glaswegians had established themselves, from Sweden to Texas, from Munich to Malaysia. Copies turned up in such august surroundings as the libraries of the House of Commons, the University of Hawaii, and many other institutions of higher knowledge. I had continued to collect vocabulary and in due course a second book was published: *The Patter – Another Blast* (Canongate, 1988). This was also highly successful, if not on the scale of the original volume.

By the time *The Patter* was ten years old I felt that my look at Glasgow language should be brought up to date and it became my goal to amalgamate the first two books and produce a compendium. The idea was to unite the best of both volumes, allow me to make amendments and update items that time had affected, and bring into print for the first time the many words and phrases that I had since compiled. This book is the fruit of that process, one I hope will appeal to readers of the preceding books as well as those who come across my work for the first time.

In these books I have always supported the idea that Glasgow language is a valid and creative dialect of Scots, not, as some would have it, a slovenly corruption of standard English. At times it seems that this battle has been fought and won; then again, a writer of the magnitude of James Kelman, an artist working at the top of his bent, of whom any national literature must be proud, can still be castigated by the ignorant for expressing himself in the demotic language of his native city. If my work contributes towards making Glaswegian Scots more respected then I will consider it to have been of some use.

I have made the point before that I am not in the business of teaching How to Speak Glaswegian; I merely wish to reflect the language that I hear and see around me. This I feel is a serious task but I know from reader reaction that this would be of limited interest without my attempts to amuse in my treatment of the material. Because of this I make no apologies for tempering scholarship with humour.

As before, the individual words are defined in alphabetical order in the body of the text. Again there are separate lists for rhyming slang and for phrases and sayings. For the first time I have included a (brief) list of Glaswegianisms that for various reasons cannot be described as current. This is in response to the large numbers of readers who wrote to me suggesting such terms, remembered from their youth in the city. While my bias will always be towards current usage, I think it worthwhile to include a few bygone expressions, especially if they seem to have escaped recording anywhere else.

Acknowledgements

It would be impossible to list here all the people who have made a contribution to this book and its predecessors. My correspondence has been voluminous, originating from all over the world, even Edinburgh, and my personal contacts stimulating and rewarding.

My thanks go now to: my father, Daniel M. Munro, without whose use and enjoyment of Glasgow dialect I would never have developed an interest in it; as ever, my wife, Alice, for never-failing encouragement and toleration; all at Canongate for their belief in the project; the citizens of Glasgow who, whether or not they realised they were doing it, supplied me with material. It's their patter.

·Apache Land·

a The word *of* often comes out like this: 'A packet a cheese an onion.'

act it Someone who is **acting it** is pretending to be innocent, trying to make another person believe that he knows nothing about what is going on: 'Don't act it, pal. Ah left a full pint standin oan the bar when Ah went tae the lavvy.'

after When a person has recently done something he may describe himself as being **just after** it: 'Naw, Ah couldny go a sweetie, hen; Ah'm just after ma dinner.' 'That's him got his books an he's just after buyin a new motor.'
What are you after? is a question that might be addressed to you in a pub. This is not a hostile or nosy enquiry but a request as to what you would like to drink.

ah but An expression introducing an objection or contradiction: 'Time you were in yer bed.' 'Ah but Mammy said we could stay up for *Father Ted*.'

ahead The phrase **go right ahead** is often used to mean have a stand-up fight with another person: 'Ootside, bawheid. You an me're gaun right ahead.'

air When something previously planned falls through or is made impossible by circumstances it may be described as being **up in the air**: 'If this snaw starts tae lie that'll be the fitba up in the air.' The phrase suggests that something has had whatever held it up removed, leaving it dangling without visible means of support, or that something has been sent flying up into the sky as if by an explosion.

airieplane An aeroplane. This is often abbreviated to **airie**: 'Moan, son, Ah'll take ye doon tae the airport an ye can watch aw the airies.'

Ally Park A nickname for Alexandra Park, a public park in the city's East End: 'Ally Park's the nearest you've ever been to the country.'

amny *or* **amn't** Local versions of *am not*: 'Ah amny comin wi yous.' 'Ah'm gettin a lift wi them, amn't Ah?'

am ur This is a strange Glasgow way of emphatically saying *I am*. It usually turns up when the speaker wants to contradict someone else: 'You're no gettin wan.' 'Am ur sot.' The negative version of this is **am urny**: 'You're gaun first.' 'No am urny.' It has been suggested that this has its origins in Gaelic but the lexicographical link has yet to be definitively established.

an at A local variant of *and that*: 'She's away tae the shoap tae get mulk an breid an at.' It is also sometimes used to refer to people as well as things: 'Ah'm gaun tae the gemme wi Chas an Doogie an Jackie an at.'

Annacker's midden A proverbial place of mess or disorder: 'Ah wid ask ye in, Mrs Eh, but they weans've got the hoose lik Annacker's midden.'

This comes from Annacker's, the name of a former firm of pork butchers, sausage makers, and ham curers. Founded in 1853, at the pinnacle of its fortunes it could boast a chain of sixteen branches all over the city. The company also owned a sausage factory, the last location of which was Napiershall

Street (near St George's Cross). The People's Palace has in its collection the shop sign from the Bridgeton Cross branch.

The theory of how this company earned a place in the dialect is as follows. Like any food retailer Annacker's had a certain amount of substandard or damaged stock that was considered unfit for sale and thrown out as refuse. It is said that the hungry poor were given to raking through Annacker's bins for anything edible and the mess this inevitably left gave rise to the phrase.

While Annacker's went out of business in 1942 the phrase the firm inspired lives on in everyday use as a perfect example of how a language clings to an expression that is vivid and memorable long after its origin is forgotten.

Annie Rooney This name is used to mean a fit of bad temper: 'If she finds out you've broken that clock she'll have an Annie Rooney.'

I don't know if this is an example of characterising the Irish as hot-tempered or if there was ever an actual person of this name. Shirley Temple starred in a 1942 film called *Miss Annie Rooney* about a poor little Irish girl, but as I have not seen this I can't say whether or not the role involved a lot of shouting the odds.

Apache land A wry description of any rough or undesirable area: 'That's real Apache land where he stays. The dugs go roon in packs for self-protection.'

appetite Someone who is eating in a particularly hearty manner may have it said of him that **he's lost his appetite and found a horse's.**

Arab A mild term of abuse: 'What are ye hingin aboot ma close fur, ya Arab?' There's nothing racist about this; it probably comes from the old use of the term 'street Arab' to describe a homeless person.

arm To **put** someone's **arm up his back** literally means to twist a person's arm behind him as a means of coercion. The phrase is often used figuratively: 'It wis his idea tae go. Naebdy put his arm up his back.'

Much stress is placed locally on not arriving empty-handed when invited to someone's house. The idea is to bring some little gift for one's host as a token of appreciation, whether this be a carefully chosen vintage wine, after-dinner mints or a bulging carry-out bag. This concept is expressed in phrases concerning the length of a guest's arms: 'Ye know oor Davie's no wan tae turn up at sumdy's door wi both erms the wan length.' 'He'd the cheek tae turn up at ma party wi wan erm as long as the other.'

arse Kick your own arse is Glasgow's more emphatic version of kick yourself: 'Imagine the big chooky tippin us the winner an no backin it hissel! He'll be kickin his own arse the night.' An inept football player may be dismissed by the phrase **he couldny kick his own arse.**

Your arse! is a robust way of saying 'I don't believe what you're telling me' and **your arse in parsley!** means much the same, if rather more poetically expressed. Other than supplying the rhyme I don't know how parsley would come to be intimate with a posterior.

A rude way of telling someone to get lost or stop annoying you is to say **away an take a run up ma arse**, secure in the belief, I'm sure, that no-one will actually comply with the instruction.

Someone who says that he detects an unpleasant odour may provoke the cheeky retort **yer nose is too near yer arse.**

If you find that another person's taste is not in harmony with your own you might be moved to say **yer taste is in yer arse.**

How's yer arse for love-bites? is the kind of disrespectful remark with which young men like to greet one another.

Someone who is very nervous or on tenterhooks may have it said of him that his **arse is nippin buttons.**

Arse, believe it or not, can also be a verb. **To arse** something is to consume or use it up quickly and greedily: 'Don't leave that gannet wi the carry-oot. He'll arse the whole lot while we're away.' Another sense is to botch something: 'He had a great chance in front of goal but the wee diddy arsed it.' This is, of course, very similar to **make an arse of** something.

arsed To say you **canny be arsed** means you can't be bothered, can't raise the necessary energy or enthusiasm: 'He wants tae go tae the pictures the night but Ah canny be arsed.'

ask for A shorthand way of sending your best wishes to someone is to instruct a mutual friend to say that you were **asking for** the person: 'If ye see Isa tell her Ah wis askin fur her.' 'Ah ran inty Wee Boaby this mornin; he wis askin fur ye.'

at This shortened form of *that* is found in various uses: 'At's terrible at, so it is.' 'Is at so?'

If you hear a cry of 'At baw!' this means that a player in a game of football has seen the ball straying in your direction and would like you to retrieve it for him.

at it Someone who is **at it** is doing something underhand or illegal: 'Keep yer eye on the guy at the till; Ah'm sure he's at it.'

aw A local version of *all*: 'Ma boots are aw mud.' 'Aye, an you can sling yer hook an aw.'

away A versatile term. Used on its own as an exclamation it indicates that the speaker doesn't believe what he has just been told: 'Ah see Aileen won the lottery.' 'Away!' A longer version of this is **away ye go!**

Away is also used in commenting on situations where something occurs that has been expected or is seen as likely to lead to further developments: 'That's her next door comin out to put her thruppence-worth in. We're away now!'

It can also mean leaving or going: 'She's away to her bed.' 'Right, I'll away then.' 'If ye're no for comin Ah'll be away masel.'

Someone who is drunk or not right in the head may be described as **away wi it**: 'You were away wi it before we even got there last night.' This is sometimes shortened to the first word alone: 'There's nae use talkin tae the bam; he's away.'

Away a place is a delicate euphemism for *dead*: 'When Ah seen that lorry wisny gauny stoap Ah thought Ah wis away a place.' It can also be used as a polite way of saying that someone has gone to the toilet: 'She'll be back in a minute. She's just away a wee place.'

Several phrases of rude dismissal begin with **away an.** Many are much too offensive to appear here but some milder examples are: **away an bile yer heid, away an pap peas at yer granny, away an play in the traffic, away an lie on yer ribs, away an peddle yer arse, away an raffle yer doughnut, away an claw yer semmit, away an play wi yersel, away an get yer heid looked!**

aye When said in an ironic tone of voice this means that you don't in the least believe what you have just been told. Sometimes **sure** is added: 'This is definitely the last time Ah'll ask ye fur a len a money.' 'Aye, sure.'

A variation is **aye, that eye** which is accompanied by pointing a finger at your own eye. The same meaning can be put across silently (handy for sharing disbelief behind the back of a third party) by simply touching your lower eyelid with your forefinger. Perhaps this is related to the old-fashioned expression 'all my eye' meaning nonsense.

Aye also turns up at the ends of queries that exemplify what might be called the Self-answered Question, e.g. 'Is that your pint, aye?' or 'You comin wi us tae Balloch, aye?' The negative of this is seen in such constructions as 'You'll no be wantin any dinner, naw?'

ayeways A local form of *always*: 'Were you ayeways so greetin-faced?'

B.1 *or* **Bee Wan** To **do a Bee Wan** means to go to another place, head off in another direction: 'When Ah seen the big moocher shufflin alang Vicky Road Ah done a Bee Wan up Torrisdale Street.'

This expression derives from a piece of civil service paperwork. When a person first registers as unemployed it is the usual practice that he receives no money for the first week from the Employment Service. If he is in need of funds he will be issued with claim form B.1 and told to use this to apply for Income Support from the Benefits Agency.

babes, the To say that something is **the babes** means that it is excellent, just what's required: 'That soup's the babes, Mammy!' An even more affectionate or appreciative version of this is **the wee babies**.

This may well be a product of rhyming slang, with *babes* being shortened from *babes in the wood*, i.e. good.

bachle *or* **bauchle** A relatively mild insult aimed at anyone

7

considered old or odd-shaped or slovenly: 'Ah'm no walkin up the road wi a wee bachle lik you!'

back The phrase **at the back of** can mean two things. The most common is in reference to time, where the back of an hour is the period just after it: 'Ah'm meetin them at the back of four.' There's no set length to this period but it would probably not extend beyond twenty minutes: 'You were meant to be here at the back of nine an it's half-nine already.'

The other use is to mean *behind*: 'She left her motor at the back of Woolies.'

All over the back is used when referring to something that is typical of a particular person: 'Wouldny gie ye the len ae a quid fur yer bus? Aye, that's him aw ower the back.' Also used by a person detecting a family resemblance between two individuals: 'He's his auld boy aw ower the back.'

backie If you help a friend climb a wall by bending over and allowing him to stand on your back you are giving him a **backie.** The same term is used when a cyclist lets someone climb on behind him on his bicycle: 'Moan Ah'll gie ye a backie up the road.'

backie-in *or* **backsie-in** In an informal game of football where one side has one more player than the other the outnumbered team may be allowed by agreement to have a **backie-in**, i.e. a player who can double as both goalkeeper and ordinary player: 'OK, yous can have Giggsy an Ah'll go backie-in fur us.'

backs The area behind a block of tenements is known as the **backs:** 'There's a pack a dugs runnin through aw the backs.' Individually, each close will have its own **back court** or **back green**: 'Aw naw, here's the rain on an Ah've got a washin oot on the back green.'

The two terms can be interchangeable but as tenements are refurbished the actual **green** or plot of grass is often replaced by a paved area.

backside furrit Backside forward, from back to front; like

8

inside out this means thoroughly or intimately: 'Never mind whit he says. Ah'm tellin ye Ah know this joab backside furrit.'

Bad Boys A disrespectful interpretation of the initials BB, standing, of course, for Boys' Brigade.

Bad Fire, the Another name for Hell: 'Ma granny says ma Uncle Joe'll go tae the Bad Fire cause he pit a foreign coin in the collection.'

bad mastard A deliberate spoonerism coined to (narrowly) avoid using foul language: 'Watch where ye're gaun wi that, ya . . . bad mastard, ye.'

badness To do something **for badness** means to do it from mere spite, to be awkward, or for mischief's sake: 'The wee horror flung hissel aff that waw fur badness just cause Ah widny pay attention tae um.'

bad turn To **take a bad turn** means to feel suddenly unwell or faint: 'Is that right your aul fella took a bad turn comin oot the subway?' This is sometimes shortened to **baddie**: 'Ah took a wee baddie this mornin an thought Ah wis fur the off.'

bag When someone is sacked from a job this is often called **being given** *or* **getting the bag**: 'It's that stupit manager should be gettin the bag, no us.'
  To bag a person is to sack him: 'That's yer last warnin, pal. Any merr a this an ye're bagged.'

-bag This is a common suffix used to label a person who epitomises the undesirable qualities of the word it is attached to, such as *crapbag* coward, or *grotbag* unpleasant or dirty person. Other such words include *shagbag* and *tossbag*.

baggies *or* **baggie-minnies** Minnows, regarded as lawful prey by children: 'Any jamjars, Maw? We're gaun fur baggies in Pollok Park.' Some people also use the term for sticklebacks.

baggy Aggie An insulting name for any female wearing ill-fitting, over-large clothes: 'Hey, baggy Aggie, did ye get that dress at Black's of Greenock?'

bag up Any drink that is very fizzy and thus fills your stomach with gas is said to **bag you up**: 'She likes that Lambrusco but Ah think it just bags ye up.' 'The wean wis that bagged up wi ginger she couldny eat her dinner.'

bahookie The backside: 'They're no makin jeans that'll go ower that big bahookie.'

baldy Someone who has had his hair cut very short may be described as having had a **baldy:** 'Tell that daft barber no tae gie ye such a baldy the next time.'

    If someone says **I haven't a baldy** this doesn't mean his hair is long but that he does not know anything about the subject being discussed: 'I asked the girl at the Information Desk but she just said "I haven't a baldy."' This is a shortened form of **a baldy clue**, meaning the slightest clue. The same adjectival use of **baldy** is found in constructions like **not a baldy one**, ie none: 'Ah went tae see if there were any biscuits in the tin. Not a baldy wan left!'

Baldy Bayne A ready-made insulting name to call a bald man: 'Who're you callin glaikit, Baldy Bayne?' Perhaps there was once a person called by this name who was well enough known to make it proverbial. At one time, certainly in the 1980s, there was a pub with this title.

baldy crust The poor old bald man gets it again with this nickname. The term is also used to mean a bald head itself: 'Ah wis near blinded wi the sun glintin aff his aul baldy crust.'

Balgray, the A familiar name for Balgrayhill, a district on the north side, near Springburn: 'Ah'd like tae go up an see ma wee niece in the Balgray but Ah'm no fit fur that hill.'

balloon A name for someone who thinks his opinions are of such value that everyone should be given the benefit of them, whereas it is obvious to the whole world that his ideas are foolish: 'Ye're in a bad way if ye pay any mind tae what that big balloon says.'

bammy Like the English version *barmy,* this means insane: 'It wis either you or wan a yer bammy pals that broke that video.'

bampot *or* **bamstick** A term applied to anyone considered 'not right in the head'. This can range from being daft to downright dangerous: 'Gauny chuck that shoutin an bawlin, ya bampot?'

Bam is a shortened version of this and turns up in the inevitable nickname for anyone called Thomas: 'Tam the Bam.'

bandit A mildly insulting name, probably a substitute used by those who don't want to say *bastard*: 'Ye've made me miss ma bus, ya bandit!'

banjo (pronounced ban-*jo*) To strike someone with one very hard blow: 'We were havin a brilliant night till bawheid decided tae banjo that bouncer.'

bar To **put the bar up** is to ban or exclude a person from a place or activity: 'His Maw flung him oot the hoose an noo his Auntie Jeannie's put the bar up as well.'

bare week A week's work without any overtime or bonus: 'Ah've tae pit in a Setterday an Sunday tae get near what he pulls in fur his bare week.'

baries To be **in one's baries** means to have nothing on your feet: 'They tiles are freezin when ye're in yer baries!'

Bar-L, the Sounding like the name of a ranch from some Western, this is actually one of the nicknames for HM Prison Barlinnie: 'He's daein his Communications Module at the Bar-L.'

barra A local version of *barrow* that appears in various phrases. Someone who thinks highly of himself may have it said of him that he **fancies his barra.** When something welcome or opportune happens to a person he may greet it by saying **that's right inty ma barra.**

A child or a small person that one feels friendly towards is often referred to as **wee barra:** 'How's it gaun the day, Wee Barra?'

The phrase **Ah've had fruit aff your barra before** is used to mean I'm once-bitten twice-shy, you don't catch me out a second time.

Barras, the The popular name for the partly open-air, partly-covered market area, east of Glasgow Cross. It is proverbially a place to find bargains, and 'Ye wouldny get *that* at the Barras' means that the purchase in question would not come cheap.

The nearby Barrowland Ballroom (known as **the Barraland**) is a famous venue for dancing and rock concerts: 'Ah huvny been tae a gig since The Pogues played the Barraland.'

bassa An altered form of *bastard*, allowing people to borrow that word's force without technically swearing: 'Ya bassa! Right on ma sore toe!' 'Ach, gie's peace ya shower a daft bassas.'

bastartin A piece of coarse language whose inventiveness lies in making a noun appear like a verb: 'Ach, chuck the bastartin thing in the bin!'

bat A punch or slap. This is most commonly found in the phrase **a bat in the mooth** which is nothing to do with eating a flying mammal but refers to a blow on the mouth: 'Tell yer pal tae watch the language or he'll be gettin a bat in the mooth.'

baw A ball, of the spherical playing variety rather than the formal dance.

Ma baw! is a cry in football uttered by a player who wants to take responsibility for playing the ball: 'If ye hear that big nutjob shoutin "Ma baw" just dive oot his road.'

The phrase **the baw's up on the slates** is an expression borrowed from street football, meaning that the ball has got stuck up on a roof and the game cannot continue. In everyday speech it is used of any situation where something has happened to make progress impossible: 'If this place isny open on a Sunday that'll be the baw up on the slates.'

To **get a kick of the baw** is another soccer-derived expression. In this case it can mean to be given an opportunity, have a chance to make a contribution: 'Aye, it'll be a different story when Labour get a kick of the baw.'

bawface A name applied to someone with a round, full face. Also used to mean such a face itself: 'Ye could see his big bawface comin a mile away.'

    Bawjaws is another, even more poetic, variation of this: 'Haw! Bawjaws! Whit aboot some service this end a the bar?'

baw-hair A pubic hair, regarded as the very narrowest of fine measures: 'Whit haunless bampot drapped that hammer? That wis a baw-hair aff stovin ma skull in!'

bawheid A mildly insulting name to address someone by: 'Watch what ye're daein wi that shovel, bawheid!' It doesn't necessarily mean that the person has a *bawface* but does imply that he is stupid, perhaps suggesting that his head is full of air like a football.

baws Balls, that is, testicles. **Yer baws!** is a fairly direct expression, meant to convey that you think someone is talking nonsense. This can be elaborated into a couple of phrases that mean the same, such as **yer baws are mince,** or **yer baws are mutton.**

bazooka'd A slang term for *drunk*: 'It's only gone nine an that tube's bazooka'd already.'

bead Someone who is drunk may be said to **have a good bead on him.**

beamer Someone whose embarrassment is made obvious by blushing is said to have a **beamer:** 'See when he got a look at hissel in the mirror . . . a pure beamer, man!' Some people like to add to a person's embarrassment by making a show of how hot the red face is. This is done by licking the index finger, holding it up and making a sizzling noise.

beans Cool the beans is an exclamation meaning calm down, take it easy, etc.: 'Hey, cool the beans, eh? It's no as bad as aw that.'

bear This word is used to mean a rowdy or aggressive young man (there seems to be no such thing as a female bear in this context): 'He's no a bad guy, jist a bit of a bear.'

Such people enjoy a good drink and a licensed establishment they patronise will acquire a reputation as a **bearpit**: 'Ah wid gie that place a bye on a Friday night if ye're no inty bearpits.'

The term **bear** is often applied to workers on a building site or an oil rig: 'He's the kind of manager that enjoys a crack with the bears after work.'

Bear With a capital letter this word means a Rangers supporter and is happily used by them, to the extent that the catering services at Ibrox offer a delicacy called Bears Pakora. It comes from the second part of the rhyming slang for Gers: *Teddy Bears*.

beardie Any bearded man will be referred to as **beardie** by the disrespectful. Also, a father tickling a child will sometimes give the child **a beardie** by rubbing his stubbly face against the child's smooth one.

beasted Someone who sets about his food in an enthusiastic, if indecorous, way is said to **get beasted in**: 'Nothin wrong wi her appetite anyway, by the way she got beasted inty that lasagne!'

beauty When a person is highly pleased by something that occurs he may mark this by crying **ya beauty**!: 'The gemme's gauny be on live? Ya beauty!'

bed-recess A feature of many traditional tenement homes, consisting of an alcove or recessed area in a living room or kitchen, originally designed to hold a bed. These beds were often boxed in and could be screened by a curtain when occupied: 'That wee bed-recess came in handy for the boy's computer desk.'

bee Someone who is seen as being absent-minded or easily confused may be called **bee-heidit**. Presumably the idea is that such a person's thoughts fly busily all over the place like bees. A similar comparison is made in the phrase **away**

wi the bees meaning the same thing: 'Where's the half-pun a butter Ah telt ye tae get? Ach, ye're away wi the bees, so ye are!'

beelin This can mean very angry: 'She tried tae keep her face straight when he telt her she wis oot the door but Ah could see she wis beelin.'

It can also be used to describe a boil or spot that looks as if it might be about to burst: 'Ye better plook that yin, it's beelin.'

beezer Anything regarded as being an excellent example of something may be called a **beezer,** but the most common local use is in referring to a very cold day: 'That wis a beezer yesterday; did your pipes freeze an aw?'

bell If someone says that he is **on the bell** this means that he reckons it is his turn to buy a round of drinks: 'Right boys, the Big Man's on the bell: what are yeez fur?'

This probably originated with the now old-fashioned pub use of push-button bells on a wall or bar-top (especially in a snug) to attract a bartender's attention.

Bella, the A nickname for Bellahouston Park, a large public park in the south-west of Glasgow, home of the Charles Rennie Mackintosh-designed Art Lover's House: 'This is a good yin of me an yer Mammy at the Bella yon time the Pope wis oan.'

It is also the nickname for Bellahouston Academy, a South-Side secondary school: 'Me'n him wis at the Bella thegither.'

belly Someone who is considered to speak without thinking or to talk a load of rubbish may have it said of him that **he just opens his mouth an lets his belly rumble.**

belong to To **belong to** a place means to live there or originate from there. The most famous example of this is the old music-hall song 'I Belong to Glasgow', but it is used to refer to specific areas too: 'Ah know that guy; he belangs tae Shettleston.'

belter Any of a wide range of things seen as exceptionally good: 'The baw landit at his feet an he hit it a belter.' 'Who wis that wee belter ye were chattin up there?'

bender mender A slang term for a stiff drink used as a hair-of-the-dog hangover cure: 'Get this doon yer thrapple. Ye look lik ye could do wi a bender mender.'

bendy juice A slang term for alcoholic drink, from the effect this has on such parts of the body as the legs.

benson A slang term for a toady or crawler: 'You're always sookin up tae the teachers, ya wee benson.' Apparently this comes from the name of the butler in *Soap*, a popular spoof TV soap opera of the late 1970s.

berries, the A term used to describe anything excellent: 'This hot weather's the berries.'

berrs, the This means the same as *the berries*, and it may be that it is simply a shortened form of it.

bet A local version of *beat*: 'Aye, we bet yeez that time an aw.' This is an example of a Glasgow pronunciation shift from the Scots *bate*.

better Two local ways of saying that something is better than nothing are:
> **better than a slap in the face wi a wet haddie**
> **better than a skelp in the baws wi a pun a wet tripe.**

bevvy Alcoholic drink is known as **the bevvy** and a single drink or a session of drinking is **a bevvy**: 'Jist cause Ah like a wee bevvy noo an then disny make us an alky or nothin.'

If one is **on the bevvy** one is in the process of drinking or has taken up drinking again after a period of abstinence: 'Two days oot the Royal an that's him back on the bevvy.' Excessive drinking is sometimes called the **heavy bevvy.**

If you like **to bevvy** (drink alcohol) you may very well end up **bevvied** (drunk), and if you are seen to do this often you might attract a reputation as a **bevvy-merchant** (not a licensed grocer but a drunkard).

Bhoys, the A nickname, supposedly indicating an Irish version of *boys,* for Celtic F. C., its players or supporters. This term is happily accepted by the club, as shown by its calling its anti-sectarian drive 'Bhoys Against Bigotry'.

biddy *or* **red biddy** A name given to any red wine that has the combination of strength and cheapness that will appeal to a down-and-out. The term is also applied to the brew resulting from mixing this with methylated spirits: 'Start drinkin that stuff an ye'll end up lyin in a skip swallyin the rid biddy.'

big This is used to mean senior or most important. The **big school** is secondary school: 'Ah'm gaun tae the big school in August.' The **big team** is the first eleven: 'The boss says Ah'll soon be ready for a run in the big team.' The **big picture** is the main feature on a cinema bill: 'Whit time's the big picture oan at?'

    Big lassie is a child's term of address to an older girl or young woman: 'Hey, big lassie, you goat the right time?'

    Big man is a friendly term of address used to someone the speaker regards as being taller than himself: 'Can Ah get a swatch at yer paper, big man?'

Big Aggie's Man A character from local mythology on whom anything you would rather not admit to can be blamed: 'It wisny me – it wis Big Aggie's Man.' The name is also used in such constructions as: 'Of course it's me. Who did ye think it was – Big Aggie's Man?'

    The original Big Aggie and her man appeared in a popular song of the 1930s.

Big Red Shed, the A nickname for the Scottish Exhibition & Conference Centre (SECC), from its factory-like red-painted exterior: 'Ageing hippies will be flocking to the Big Red Shed when Neil Young and Crazy Horse attempt to lift the roof in July.'

Billy *or* **Billy-boy** A nickname for a Protestant, especially a supporter of Glasgow Rangers F. C., many of whom use it to introduce themselves: 'Hullo! Hullo! We are the Billy-boys.'

This goes back to King William III (originally William of Orange), the military hero of Protestantism.

binger pronounced to rhyme with *singer*, this is a word used by betting enthusiasts for a losing bet: 'He had five lines on this morning an every wan a binger.'

binnies A familiar term for binmen or refuse collectors: 'She always leaves out a few cans of beer for the binnies at Christmas.'

birlin A Scots word meaning *spinning*, often used locally to mean drunk: 'Sumdy'll need tae see Gus up the road. The man's birlin.' There are a couple of more elaborate forms of this, such as 'His eyes are birlin' or 'The eyes are birlin in his heid.'

biscuit tin The proverbial place of safe-keeping for the funds of Celtic F. C.: 'Fergus McCann will have to dig deep in the biscuit tin to cover this latest plunge into the transfer market.'

bit A local word for one's home, or home area: 'Emdy fancy comin back tae ma bit?'

To **take the bit out of** someone is to exhaust him, leave him out of breath: 'These stairs of yours fair take the bit out of me.'

When it comes to the bit means at the vital moment: 'That wee waster'll always let ye down when it comes to the bit.'

black-affronted An almost poetic description of the state of being extremely embarrassed or offended: 'Imagine ma ain daughter-in-law no lettin me in her hoose! Black-affrontit wasny in it!'

Black Street The proverbial name and location of a clinic that is, amongst other things, a treatment centre for venereal disease: 'Ah wis just tellin yer girlfriend here that Ah've no seen ye since Ah bumped inty ye at Black Street the other week.' A dreadful insult, whose implications will be obvious, is to call someone a **Black Street case.**

bladder A term used for a football that is a proper leather one, as opposed to one made of plastic: 'It's no joke tryin tae heidie a soakin-wet muddy bladder.'

bladdered A slang term for drunk.

blast A taste or portion of something, particularly of alcoholic drink: 'See's another blast a that malt, big yin.'

blaw The Scots word for blow, used locally as a slang term for marijuana: 'Is he bevvied or what?' 'Naw, too much a the blaw.'

It can also mean an instance of partaking of said weed: 'Ah huvny hud a wee blaw fur ages, man.'

blitzed Yet another word meaning drunk: 'Let's get blitzed again, like we did last summer.'

bloodsucker A children's name for a big fat earthworm: 'Ah goat a big bloodsucker fae under a plank an stuck it doon his collar.'

blooter One of the many terms that have come from football into general use. To **blooter** the ball in a game is to kick it powerfully but without much control: 'How could ye no have squared it tae me instead a blooterin it inty the crowd?' The verb can also mean to do something in a quick and careless way: 'There's no way that hoose could be painted right in wan day; they must've blootered it.' Similarly, if a person very quickly spends a sum of money he may be said to have 'blootered the whole lot'.

A **blooter** is a powerful but unskilful kick of a ball: 'Will Scottish defenders never tire of the big blooter up the park?' It also means a quickly done, sloppy job: 'Look at the runs in this paintwork; this's been a blooter of a job.'

Someone who is very drunk may be described as being **blootered.**

blue Rangers F. C. customarily play in blue shirts and various nicknames they are known by are testimony to this, such as **the Light Blues** or **the boys in (royal) blue.**

19

blue job A slang term for a five-pound note: 'That wis a blue job Ah gave ye, by the way, no a wancer.'

bluenose Because of the team colours, this is a nickname for a supporter of Rangers F. C.: 'We worked thegither for years an Ah never knew he wis such a bluenose.'

Blythswood Square An area of the city that is highly respectable and businesslike during the day and proverbial for being frequented by prostitutes at night: 'An where d'ye think ye're gaun dressed lik that: Blythswood Square?'

boady A local version of *body*. **Gie's a boady!** is a cry sometimes heard at football matches when a fan reckons his team's defenders are not exhibiting total commitment in the tackle. In the 1960s there was a TV Western series that featured a hero called Cheyenne Bodie. This person would be addressed by Mexicans as 'Señor Bodie', inspiring wacky funsters to make the suggestive crack: 'Seen yer boady!'

boat The phrase **just off the boat** implies that a person so described is a recent immigrant from Ireland and is therefore stereotyped as naive and unsophisticated in the ways of the western metropolis. It is often applied to those who have a look of being of Irish descent: 'Is that her aul fella? He looks like he's just off the boat.'

body swerve Another term from football, where it means the act of getting past an opposing player by a quick movement of the whole body out of his reach. In general parlance it is used to mean any kind of avoiding action, any instance of getting out of doing something: 'Ah'm that knackered Ah think Ah'll just gie the night class a body swerve.' It can also be used as a verb: 'Fancy body-swervin the union meetin an nickin oot for a pint?' This can occur in the shortened form, **swerve:** 'Ah never saw ye at the aul dear's party: how'dye manage tae swerve that?'

bogey[1] The phrase **the game's a bogey** means that because a deadlock or stalemate has been reached (or some other

20

reason has made it impossible to continue) the proceedings in question can go no further: 'If that's yer final offer the game's a bogey.'

This comes originally from the phrase's use in children's games when said by a player who decides the game isn't fair or can't be played properly to the end.

bogey² A local name for a child's cart (if such continue to be made) constructed from a wooden box or odd pieces of wood, made mobile by the attachment of pram wheels.

boggin A term applied to anything considered foul-smelling: 'Get they shoes oot the bedroom; they're pure boggin!'

boilermaker A disparaging name for a doctor who is regarded as being insufficiently gentle in his handling of patients' bodies: 'That's never a doactor, that. He's a boilermaker.'

boke Vomit. To **boke** is to be sick: 'If ye're gauny boke, gauny try an make it tae the lavvy?' It can also mean to make someone feel sick: 'That would boke ye, wouldn't it no?' If something disgusts you, you might say it **gives you the boke.** If the thing or person in question is particularly nauseating you might add the word **dry** to this, suggestive of dry retching: 'Don't mention that wummin in ma company; it gies me the dry boke jist thinkin aboot her.'

Boke also means the physical product of vomiting: 'How come there's a pile of boke at this corner every Sunday morning?'

Someone who is feeling nauseous may be described as feeling or being **boky**: 'Make sure ye get a windy seat for Wee Boky.' If you are **boky-fu** you have made yourself feel sick by drinking too much or overeating.

bold To put the words **the bold** before a person's name can be a way of saying that you think he is cheeky or pushy, although this is often used ironically to mean exactly the opposite: 'Well, if it isny the bold Arthur! Is it no past your bedtime, son?'

bomb To **bomb** (something or someone) **out** means to reject it or him: 'Did ye see the look she gave him? That's him bombed out there!' 'How is it every idea I put to the committee gets bombed out?'

bonnie A bonfire: 'Mister, kin we go through your skip fur stuff fur wur bonnie?'

books To **get** *or* **be given one's books** is to be dismissed from a job: 'When he turned up on the Monday morning they just gave him his books.'

boolin, the The game of bowling or an occasion of this: 'He's wantin his good blazer dry-cleaned for the boolin.'

boona To **give it the full boona** means to go the whole hog, hold nothing back, particularly in a situation in which you may as well be hung for a sheep as a lamb: 'Are ye for the off after this pint or are we gauny gie it the full boona the night?'

This term entered the dialect from Indian and Pakistani restaurants where if you order a dish called a boona (as in a lamb boona, etc.) the sauce is thicker and drier than in a standard curry. In some restaurants it is possible to order a half boona or a full boona, depending on how the size of your eyes relates to that of your belly.

boot To **boot** someone can mean to sack him: 'Whit're you daein back here? Did Ah no tell ye ye're booted?'

To **put** or **stick the boot on** a person is to kick him: 'Ah seen two boays puttin the boot oan an old jakey.'

Boots' Corner Although the corner of Argyle Street and Union Street is no longer occupied by Boots the Chemist, this handy place for dating couples to meet is still referred to by the old name. It is also known as **Dizzy Corner.**

booze cruise A pleasure cruise down the Clyde or on a loch or canal during which it is understood there will be substantial splicing of the mainbrace. Far from trying to live down such a nickname, some companies offering the service actually use the term in their advertising.

boss In some schools, a nickname for the headmaster: 'C'mon, here's the boss comin!'

bothy This rural term for a shepherd's hut or farm workers' bunkhouse is used in urban contexts for any temporary shelter for workmen, including the portable constructions that have electricity, running water, and telephones. It is even used to mean the workers' cloakroom/toilet area in a factory: 'Ah don't care if it's chuckin it doon; youse're no peyed tae sit playin kerds in this bothy aw day!'

bought house A home that is privately owned rather than rented: 'Ma son an his wife are gettin on great – they stay in a bought hoose noo, ye know.'

bowf If something is very smelly it may be described as **bowfin:** 'Ah'll need tae clean oot that fridge; there's somethin bowfin in there.'

A **bowf** is a stink or nasty smell and a particularly sickening example of this is often called a **honkin bowf.**

bowfies A local term for head lice: 'Miss, can Ah no sit next tae him? His heid's full a bowfies, so it is.' There must be a connection between this and *bowf.*

bowly Pronounced so that the 'bow' rhymes with 'cow', this means bandy-legged: 'Ah'm gaun bowly wi humphin that wean up the stair.'

box Used as a slang term for the head in such phrases as **out ma box** which means very drunk or incapacitated by drugs. If something **does your box in** this means it is beyond your powers of understanding: 'Miss, they irregular verbs are pure daein ma box in; could ye no read us a story?'

brain Someone who is described as being **out his brain** is totally intoxicated: 'Ah canny remember gettin hame last night. Must've been right oot ma brain.' **Brainless** is used in a similar way.

A contemptuous way of referring to a no-scoring draw in football is to say **nae brains each.**

brammed-up Dressed up in your best gear, done up to the nines: 'Is this you away hame tae get brammed-up fur the dancin the night?' This is obviously related to *brammer*.

brammer A term applied to anything considered a first-class example of its kind: 'Ye should see his new motor; what a brammer!'

bran new A versatile term of approval. It can mean healthy, feeling fine: 'How're ye this mornin?' 'Bran new!' Used of a person it can also mean friendly, nice, dependable, etc.: 'Ye don't have tae worry aboot Rick. He's bran new, that guy.' It is also used as a general term of reassurance: 'Can Ah get ye a drink?' 'Naw, ye're bran new, pal, Ah'm gettin them.'

brassneck To **brassneck it** is to try to get away with something by a show of sheer confidence and nerve: 'If they ask ye for yer ticket just brassneck it an say ye're with the band.'

bree A local word for *brother*: 'Is it okay if Ah bring the wee bree?'

breenge Someone who **breenges** rushes recklessly: 'Ye've got tae make an appointment. Ye canny just breenge in an see them.'
   A **breenge** is an example of doing this. 'Now I don't want a mad breenge for the door when the bell goes.'
   Someone who behaves impetuously may be called a **breenger.**

breidsnapper A slang term for a child, emphasising the aspect of a constant necessity to keep it fed: 'Ah haveny been tae Girvan since Ah wis a breidsnapper.' This is sometimes shortened to **snapper.**

brekwist A local variant of breakfast. How the *f* became a *w* is anybody's guess: 'Ah like a bit a bacon fur ma brekwist oan ma hoalidays.'

brick A slang term for a pound sterling: 'Gauny stake us a brick tae the morra?'

bricks If someone is described as being **in with the bricks** this doesn't mean he is on good terms with the building blocks but that the person in question has been present in a company or establishment since its beginning.

brig This is the Scots word for *bridge* and forms part of a few place names and street names in and around Glasgow, such as The Briggait (the road to the bridge) and Brigton (Bridgeton).

broken pay A wage-packet that has been opened and had some of the money extracted and spent. Traditionally, in households where the woman handles the finances, the wage-earner will be expected to come straight home after work with the packet intact to be handed over to her. Males of more dauntless mind might head for the pub first and spend some of their wages there before going home. A fearsome or dominant woman may have it said of her: 'Ye wouldny want tae go hame tae her wi a broken pay.'

broo *or* **buroo** A slang term for the Employment Service: 'He's away doon the broo for a restart interview.' This comes from the local pronunciation of *bureau* in Employment Bureau, an earlier name for this government department. Unemployment Benefit is known as **broo money.** Someone who is signing on to receive this is said to be **on the broo.**

bubble To **bubble** is to cry: 'If ye stop yer bubblin Daddy'll maybe get ye a new wan.' A spell of crying may be called a **bubble**: 'When Ah fun that aul photie Ah jist had tae sit doon an have a wee bubble tae masel.'

Bubbly is a term applied to someone who is crying or in a bad mood: 'What's up wi your face, bubbly?'

The **Bubbly Babies** (crybabies) is cheeky name for the BB (Boy's Brigade).

bucket This can mean a bin: 'The bucket is all that's good for.' To **bucket** something is to throw it out, reject it as not good enough: 'Give me one good reason why I shouldn't just bucket this essay.'

A **bucket** can also mean a large amount of alcohol: 'You must've had a right bucket last night to end up in a state like this.' Someone who regularly drinks heavily may have it said of him that he **takes a good bucket.**

Buckie[1] A familiar name for Buchanan Street: 'Ah seen her runnin up Buckie headin for Queen Street Station.'

Buckie[2] A nickname for *Buckfast*, a proprietory brand of cheap and strong tonic wine: 'Ah'm no sayin the boozer wis a bit downmarket, but Ah've never seen Buckie in an optic before.'

buckie-up Another term, like **backie**, meaning the use of one's back to help someone to climb: 'Ah could get up there if wanny yeez wid gie us a buckie-up.'

bug To **let bug** is to divulge information, let others in on something not generally known: 'The fly aul devil backs a lottery ticket every week an never lets bug tae her.'

bug-ladders Sideburns, the cheeky implication being that the wearer is infested: 'How d'ye no just let yer bug-ladders grow thegither an cry it a beard?'

Bully Wee, the A nickname for Clyde F. C., who formerly played at Shawfield and now are based at Broadwood, near Cumbernauld. The 'bully' part of the name simply means 'good' (as in 'bully for you'). The club is 'wee' in that it is not on the same level of wealth and importance as the Old Firm.

bum A **bum** is a boaster, someone who goes on endlessly about himself, his doings or his possessions: 'And you told me you'd done this sort of thing before. You're nothing but a bum.'

To **bum** is to boast, make empty claims: 'Away ye go, ye're bummin!' To **bum your chaff** *or* **load** is to use your line of patter to talk someone round or pull a fast one on him: 'Ye'd think he was loaded to hear him bummin his chaff.'

To **bum** (something) **up** means to praise something, claim that it is excellent: 'That picture wis bummed up tae be the greatest thing since *Whisky Galore* an here it wis mince.' 'He can bum hissel up aw he likes an Ah'm still no impressed.'

bumfle When a piece of material or a garment is **bumfled** this means it is wrinkled or creased: 'Get aff us, you, you're gauny get ma good dress aw bumfled.' A **bumfle** is a crease or wrinkle: 'You can smooth out the bumfles in that tablecloth instead of sitting there like a dumpling.'

bummer A rather disrespectful term for a manager or other figure of authority is **heid bummer**: 'Her aul man's wan a the heid bummers in Weir's.'

bump[1] Another word for the sack, dismissal from your employment: 'Ah see wee Doogie goat the bump fae his work the other week.'

bump[2] A slang word meaning to swindle, fiddle, defraud: 'He used tae be a Pools collector till he got caught bumpin the money.'

bun For some reason this is used as an insult for a woman considered unattractive or of dubious reputation: 'Seen the wee man's latest girlfriend? A pure bun!'

bunnit Most commonly this is a man's cloth cap, but the term can also be used for other types of hat. In his routine about the Crucifixion Billy Connolly coined the name 'jaggy bunnit' for the crown of thorns placed on Christ's head.

To **do your bunnit** means to become extremely angry: 'He's gauny do his bunnit if he disny find that ticket.'

The term **bunnit-hustler** was invented in the 1970s as a disparaging term for someone who plays up his humble working-class origins, especially one who does this from the comfortable position of being currently well-off or successful.

burny Very hot to the touch or taste: 'Mind that hot iron, son ... burny, burny!' 'Can Ah get anither wan a yer sweeties, wan a the burny wans?'

buroo A variant form of **broo**.

burst To **burst** someone is to give him a physical beating. It is also found in the more specific threat: 'Ah'll burst yer arse!'

To **burst** a bank-note is to use some of its value to pay for something: 'Ye canny burst a twinty for a paper.' 'Ah feel that reckless Ah could burst a fiver!'

If a betting line or pools coupon is **burst** this means it has been made a loser by some element of the betting choice: 'That's me finished wi St Mirren; two weeks in a row they've went an burst ma coupon.'

Someone who is in dire need of a visit to the toilet may be described as **burstin**: 'Let us in quick! Ah'm burstin!' This may be elaborated by describing the particular form of relief required, as in 'Ah'm burstin fur a slash!'

bus The cry **haud the bus!** means wait a minute, slow down, don't be hasty: 'Here, haud the bus. Yer shirt tail's hingin oot.'

Someone who is referring to a sum of money so small as to be insignificant may say **Ah've lost merr runnin for a bus.**

but[1] An unusual local form of contradiction involves adding this to the end of a statement: 'She wants tae go tae East Kilbride. Ah'm no fur movin but.' In similar constructions **but** takes the place of the standard English 'though' or 'however': 'The dinners areny up tae much. Dead cheap but.'

This formation is found in Australian English too, no doubt imported along with exiles from this part of the world.

but[2] A local version of *bit* or *bitten*: 'Your dug's just but ma leg.'

buttie *or* **buttie-up** A walk in the company of an acquaintance: 'Haud on a wee minute an Ah'll gie ye a buttie up the road.'

buzz To **buzz** is to sniff glue or other solvents: 'The boay's oot his brain buzzin hauf the time.'

bye If you **give** something **a bye** this means you refrain from doing it: 'They're aw gaun tae the gemme the night but Ah reckon Ah'll gie it a bye.' 'Ah thought Ah tellt yeez tae gie that shoutin an bawlin a bye!' This comes from the football usage where a team may be given a bye, i.e. be allowed to go through to the next round of a competition without having to play a qualifying game, because there is an odd number of contesting sides.

bye kick A goal kick in football: 'The keeper let it go for a bye kick.'

That's you clamped!

cady A man's hat: 'He left his good cady on the subway.'

cakey A fairly mild word used to describe someone regarded as daft, not all there: 'Did you give him the len of a tenner? You're cakey, so ye are!' Like *doughheid* this seems to have something to do with baking. Perhaps the idea is that a foolish person's head is like risen dough: full of nothing but air.

Cally *or* **Carly** Nicknames for Carlsberg Special, a proprietary brand of strong lager: 'That's three heavies, two Callies, an a vodka an Irn Bru.'

cally dosh A slang term for money: 'Naw, Ah'm stayin in the night – a slight problem wi the cally dosh.'

canny This means can't: 'Ye canny shove yer granny aff a bus.'

cargo A slang word for carry-out: 'Ye should a seen the size a the cargo they turnt up wi!'

carry-out A **carry-out** is an amount of food or alcoholic drink bought in one place to be consumed somewhere else. The standard English form is *takeaway*. 'That lassie just lifted a bottle out your carry-out.' 'His idea of a cooked breakfast is microwaving the remains of last night's Indian carry-out.'

The term is also used for a takeaway restaurant: 'Everything's shut except the Chinese carry-out.' A **carry-out bag** is the type of plastic bag pubs supply for takeaway booze, usually emblazoned with a brewer's logo: 'Can you not find something better for your swimming stuff than that old carry-out bag?'

The fact that local pronunciation is often *cairry-oot* or *kerry-oot* has led me to wonder if the name of a pub I once came across, The Kerry Inn, was intended as a pun.

cattie Short for catalogue, particularly as used in mail-order shopping: 'Did ye get that coat oot the cattie?'

caunle A candle: 'Ah'm no sayin she's gettin auld, but when they lit the caunles oan her birthday cake it set aff the smoke alarm.'

caur This was formerly used to mean a tramcar (collectively known as **the caurs**) but nowadays it refers to a motor car. It is a good example of the local tendency to pronounce the *ar* sound as *aur*. 'It's no faur tae Baurrheid if ye've goat a caur.'

caw If you **caw the legs** *or* **feet** from a person you sweep his legs out from under him. Unsurprisingly, this comes up time and again in football contexts: 'Caw the legs fae that big diddy!'

Celts, the Pronounced *selts*, this is one of the nicknames for Celtic F. C.: 'Oh when the Celts go marchin in . . .'

Central Glasgow Central Station: 'Ah'll get ye at Central at half seven, ootside R. S. McColl's'

cerd (pronounced *kerd*) A local variant of *card*: 'Ah pit ma cerd in that puggy a yours an it swallied it.'

chant To sing: 'She's been makin a few bob daein a wee bit a chantin round the pubs.' A **chanter** is a singer: 'She's a rare wee chanter, that lassie.'

chanty-wrastler A mild insult composed of two venerable Scots words: **chanty** meaning a chamberpot, and **wrastler** meaning wrestler. 'Tell the aul chanty-wrastler tae go tae his bed an gie us aw peace.' The implication could be that the insultee is as despicable as a servant who empties chamberpots. It was also suggested to me (by a Professor of English Literature, no less) that the term might describe someone who fastidiously manoeuvres the chanty so as to pee round the rim and thus avoid making a noise. The truth must be out there.

chap **To chap** is to knock, like Wee Willie Winkie: 'Chappin at the windae.' In the game of dominoes if a player says he is **chapping** this means he is unable to use any of his pieces and has to miss a turn. The player will often signal this by chapping on the table.

In phrases like 'There was a chap at the door' the **chap** is not an unspecified person but a knock.

character The phrase **give someone his character** means to tell the person exactly what you think of him, never very complimentary: 'She fair gied him his character when he sobered up.'

check When someone wants to draw something particular to your attention he may do so using a phrase beginning with this word: 'Check the suit, boys.' 'Check that wee bird in the red.'

cheekywatter A nickname for alcoholic drink, highlighting its property of making some people bumptious and at the same time dismissing its effects as none too serious: 'The booze is only cheekywatter tae them. They're inty other stuff fur a real buzz.'

chib A **chib** is a sharp-edged weapon, such as a knife or a razor. **To chib** a person is to use such a weapon on him. Someone who is known to use a blade in fighting may be called a **chib-merchant**. A **chib-mark** is a scar, as from the wound of a knife or razor: 'Check that for a hard ticket, eh? Chib-marks aw ower the coupon.'

chiefie A friendly term of address for a male stranger, or an affectionate nickname for a pal: 'Ye finished wi that paper, chiefie?'

chin To **chin** a person is to stop him and speak to him: 'Chin that stewardess for another cup of coffee, will you?'

choke To **choke down** something means to drink it despite having difficulty in swallowing, usually because you have already had enough to drink or it tastes unpleasant: 'See him an his home-made wine? If ye manage tae choke doon wan gless he thinks ye're wantin anither wan.'

On the other hand, to **choke** a bottle is to drink it quickly: 'The perr a them were chokin a bottle a tequila.'

chokin In dire need of a drink: 'Any danger of some service up this end a the bar? There's guys chokin up here.'

chookie A **chookie** *or* **chookiebirdie** is a bird, in the kind of vocabulary an adult would use to a child: 'Aw, look at the wee chookiebirdies eatin the breid.'

Chookie is also used to mean a stupid person: 'Think ye can make me look lik a chookie an get away wi it?' The word also appears in phrases that contradict a previous statement: 'He says he'll take it with him.' 'Will he chookie!'

chow Pronounced to rhyme with *cow*, this means to chew: 'Ah'm no sayin the soup wis too thick but ma jaws are sore wi chowin it.'

chuck The phrase **gie it a chuck** means to desist, stop doing a particular thing: 'Gauny gie that whingein a chuck?'

chute A playground slide for children: 'That chute's no awfy slidey.'

Citz, the An affectionate nickname for the Citizens' Theatre: 'What's on at the Citz on Saturday?'

claim To **claim** a person is to accost him in one of various ways. It can mean to greet someone in a friendly manner: 'I thought I wasn't going to know anybody at the party but Sheila claimed me as soon as I went in the door.' It can involve a little less friendliness: 'Here's Joey comin. Ah'm gauny claim him for that tenner he owes me.'

It can also be downright hostile, indeed a challenge to a fight: 'Hey bawheid! You're claimed!'

clamp If you tell someone to **clamp it** you are saying be quiet, shut your mouth: 'You've got a big mouth for a wee boy, haven't ye, son? Well, clamp it!'

If you deliver what you consider to be an unanswerable retort to an adversary in an argument you might say: 'That's you clamped.'

clapped-in A term used to describe a face that is thin or shrunken-looking: 'That's her faither over there: the wee aul guy wi the clapped-in jaws.' If a person tastes something very sour or hot and the experience makes him suck in his cheeks a similar expression is used: 'Try a mouthful of this. That'll clap yer jaws in for ye.'

clappy-doo Sometimes seen in local fish shops, this is a kind of large black mussel. The word is often shortened to **clappy**: 'Ye get the best wulks an clappies at that wee place near the Barras.' The term is a variation of the Gaelic *clab*, meaning an enormous mouth, and *dubh*, meaning black.

Clarence A nickname for a person with crossed eyes: 'What's Clarence's right name anyway?' This comes from a crosseyed lion of the same name, star of a popular 1960s television series called *Daktari*.

clatty *or* **clarty** This means dirtied with mud or just plain dirty: 'Don't you dare tramp ma good carpet wi they clatty boots on.' 'Ye should see the state a his hair: pure clatty-lookin.'

A **clat** is a term used for a person considered dirty: 'The wee clat picked a sweetie up aff the grun an et it.'

Clenny, the A familiar name for the City of Glasgow Council Cleansing Department: 'Are you gauny tidy up that bedroom or dae Ah have tae phone up the Clenny tae come an clear it?'

A **clenny-motor** is a bin lorry: 'We couldny get up the lane for that big clenny-motor.'

click To **get a click** means to meet and establish a relationship with a member of the opposite sex: 'C'mon we'll go to the dancin; ye're no too old yet to get a click.'

Clockwork Orange A nickname, perhaps more popular in the media than in the street, for the Subway. This dates only from its reopening in 1979, after modernisation, when the trains appeared in a new orange livery.

close In a tenement building the common entrance and hall is known as a **close**: 'The dug's ran up that close'. 'She stays up the next close.' The term is also used to mean all the individual flats and their occupants considered as a unit: 'She cleans the stairs for the whole close.'

The phrase **up the wrang close** is sometimes used to mean in error, barking up the wrong tree: 'If that's what ye think, ye're up the wrang close.'

The **close-mouth** is the street entrance of a close. The **back-close** is the rear area of a close: 'Mind we used tae dae wur winchin up a back-close?'

cloy up This means to shut up, to stop speaking: 'Gauny cloy up, you?' It is a variation of *clay up*, meaning to seal a hole or gap with clay.

cludgie A familiar term for a toilet, sometimes shortened to **cludge**: 'What's keepin you in that cludgie? Writin yer memoirs?'

clug To **clug** or **put the clug on** someone, especially in a football game, is to kick him: 'Put the clug on that wee bam!'

Clyde Glasgow's river features in many catchphrases. The most popular involves asking someone if he thinks you are stupid by saying **do you think I came up the Clyde on a bike?** The bike can be substituted by other unlikely modes of navigating the river, such as **a banana boat, a coolie boat, a wheelbarrow,** and **a watter biscuit.**

Someone who is considered unusually fortunate may have

it said of him that **he could fall inty the Clyde an come up wi a fish supper** _or_ **wi his pockets full a fish.**

The question **what's that got to do wi Clyde navigation?** is a fancy way of saying 'what's that got to do with the subject of discussion?' or 'I fail to see the relevance of that.'

Co, the A nickname for a store owned by the Co-operative Wholesale Society: 'She always buys her messages out the Co.' A peculiarity of Glasgow pronunciation is that the full word 'co-operative' is often pronounced coaper*ai*tive.

coal-carry A local name for a piggyback: 'Moan, wee man. Ah'll gie ye a coal-carry if ye stoap greetin.' The obvious comparison being made is that the person given this is carried like a sack of coal on a coalman's back.

coffin end The narrow end of a tenement building that is tapered (something like a coffin in shape) rather than rectangular: 'The hooses are always wee an poky in a coffin end.'

colour Used as a standard of dirtiness, especially of a garment or a person: 'Look at the colour of your shirt. Manky!' 'Ye should've seen the colour of him when he came in after playin fitba.'

come ahead A phrased used when trying to make someone see sense or change their behaviour: 'Is that aw ye've done? Aw come ahead, will ye?' It is also a form of challenge to fight: 'Think ye're hard, eh? Come ahead then.'

come away A cry of encouragement: 'Come away the Spiders!'

coo's arse A term used to describe any mess or botched job: 'Whoever hung this wallpaper made a coo's arse of it.' Used in particular to mean the end of a cigarette that has been over-moistened by the smoker's saliva: 'OK, ye can have a drag a ma fag but don't gie it a coo's arse.'

cop To **cop your whack** is to partake of something, whether it be your share, something to eat or drink, or even a good look at something worth seeing: 'Cop yer whack fur a bacon roll before they're aw gone.' 'Here she comes noo. Cop yer whack for *that*!'

The phrase can also mean to die: 'Her aul boy copped his whack at Monte Cassino.'

corrie-fistit Someone described as **corrie-fistit** is left-handed. A left-handed person is sometimes called a **corrie-fister.**

country pancake A kids' term for a cow's dropping: 'What would ye rather do . . . run a mile, jump a stile, or eat a country pancake?'

coup *or* **cowp** To **coup** something is to spill it, knock it over, or dump it: 'The big eejit's went an couped the milk jug aw ower the good tablecloth.' 'She sat on the edge of the table an cowped the hale lot.' 'See if Ah get the guy that's coupin his rubbish in that back lane . . . ?'

To **coup out** is to fall asleep or otherwise lose consciousness: 'When Ah got up on Sunday Ah fun two guys couped out on the kitchen flerr.'

A **coup** is a rubbish dump: 'Ah'm away tae the coup wi these hedge clippins.' The term is also used for any particularly untidy place: 'That livin room's a pure coup wi aw your toys.'

coupon A slang term for a person's face: 'He had that big daft grin all over his coupon.'

crap To **crap it** means to be scared or lose your nerve: 'Ah wis crappin it in case embdy seen us.' A more elaborate form of this is **crap your load**. To **crap it off** a person or thing is to be particularly scared of him or it: 'Everybody knows you're crappin it aff the gaffer.'

To call someone a **crapper** or a **crap-bag** is to call him a coward: 'Want tae make somethin of it, ya crapper?'

crash To **crash the lights** is to deliberately fail to stop at a traffic light that has just turned red: 'Hell mend ye . . . it's yer ain fault fur crashin the lights.'

To **crash ahead** means to carry on with a task without delay: 'You crash ahead wi the undercoatin till Ah get this door-frame sanded.'

crater-face An unkind name to call a person whose face is pockmarked or scarred by acne: 'It's no make-up crater-face wants . . . it's Polyfilla.'

craw To **craw it,** like **crap it,** is to be afraid. Similarly, a **crawbag** is someone who is afraid.

cream cookie A cake, consisting of a sweet bun split and filled with (usually artificial) cream: 'Ah could go a cream cookie wi ma tea, or maybe a wee French fancy.'

cremmy A slang term for crematorium: 'It wis hellish tryin tae get parked ootside that cremmy.'

cuff¹ To defeat, especially in a convincing manner: 'Aye, your team was well cuffed the day.'

cuff² A collective term for unattached and therefore presumably available women: 'No much ae a party that. There were nae cuff at aw.' Possibly this derives from rhyming slang for stuff, as in *bit of stuff.*

curer An alcoholic drink taken the morning after a drinking session, intended to dispel the effects of a hangover: 'C'mon for a wee curer an ye'll be bran new.'

Curry Alley A nickname for Gibson Street, in the West End, famous for its large number of curry restaurants in what is a relatively short street.

curry-shop A familiar term for any Indian or Pakistani restaurant: 'Anybody know a curry-shop that does home deliveries?'

cutter To **run the cutter** means to act as a bookie's runner or take someone else's line to the betting-shop for him. Apparently this comes from an older use of the phrase referring to smugglers evading the cutter (boat) of the revenue officers.

cut-up A dishonest or fixed outcome to such events as competitions, elections, dividends, or job applications: 'You'd hee-haw chance of gettin that job; it was a cut-up from the start.'

Look at dreamy Daniel gawpin oot the windae. Must be love, eh?

da Father: 'Is that your da waitin at the bus-stop?' 'Want a wee hand wi they messages, Da?'

dabbity A transfer, that is, a design printed on glossy paper that when licked and applied to the back of a child's hand will leave an image on the skin: 'Call that a tattoo? Ah've seen better dabbities.'

    The word probably derives from the action of dabbing at the transfer on one's hand to make it print properly.

dale At a swimming pool, **the dale** is the high diving board or platform: 'Gaun! Ye're feart tae dive the dale!'

    This probably comes from the local pronunciation of *deal*, the wood often used to make such boards, in the same way that *beat* is often pronounced *bate*.

Dale, the A nickname for Leverndale psychiatric hospital: 'Did ye no know he's been in an oot the Dale for years?'

Dallie, the A familiar name for the Dalmarnock area, in the

East End: 'Ah comes aff the plane at Toronto, an ye know who wis the customs man? Wee Charlie fae the Dallie!'

damage A jocular term for a person's activity or doings, especially relating to someone enjoying himself in a boisterous manner: 'Naw, Ah'm no fur gaun hame yet – Ah've a lot merr damage tae dae the night.'

damp, dampt Words used as substitutes for *damn, damned* by those who don't like to be heard to swear: 'Ye've just stood on ma dampt toe, ya stupit-lookin clown ye!'

Dan Nickname for a Roman Catholic: 'Are ye a Billy or a Dan or an aul tin can?'

dancer[1] A slang term for a landing or floor in a tenement building, e.g. a **three-dancer** is the third floor; a **four-dancer** is the fourth floor: 'How is it whenever Ah've tae deliver a new machine it's always a four-dancer?'

A **tap-dancer** is, of course, not a variety turn in this context but the top (*tap*) floor.

dancer[2] Ya dancer is an exclamation of joy or enthusiastic approval: 'That's us fixed up for the holidays! Ya dancer!'

danger This word is used ironically to mean possibility or chance when it appears that the event referred to is not likely to happen: 'D'ye think there's any danger of your wee brother turnin up on time?' 'Any danger of gettin served the night?'

The phrase **no danger** is used to confirm that something is sure to take place: 'Ye'll definitely come an get us?' 'No danger, wee man; Ah'll be there!'

daud *or* **dod** Any piece or portion of something: 'Want a daud a breid wi yer soup?' 'A big dod a concrete fell aff that buildin an nearly kilt an aul wummin.' The bus company Dodds of Troon unwittingly provides innocent amusement as generations of Glasgow humorists have visualised pieces of the seaside resort bowling along the road.

dauner A **dauner** is a leisurely walk or stroll: 'Fancy a wee dauner doon tae the Toll an back?' **To dauner** is to take such a walk: 'Ah bumped inty yer folks daunerin doon Albert Drive.'

Davie Dunnit A slang term for the kind of individual who always claims to have equalled, if not bettered, the achievements of anyone else: 'Ah canny go that guy at aw; he's a right Davie Dunnit.'

dead *or* **deid** In a bar, an unfinished drink that has been abandoned by its drinker is often described as **dead**: 'Ye can clear these tumblers away, barman; they're aw dead except this yin.'

dearie mearie A mild exclamation, being a local (and more poetic) variant of *dear me*.

deck **The deck** means the floor or the ground: 'Who left ma good jaiket lyin on the deck?'

    To deck someone is to knock him down with a blow: 'Rab jist got up an decked the ignorant pig.'

    To be decked is to be laughing so much that you are in danger of falling over: 'We were aw pure decked when we clocked ye wi yer new suit oan.'

deefie A cheeky name to call someone who fails to heed what he is told, or is in fact deaf: 'Hey deefie! Did ye no hear me shoutin on ye?'

    To **throw** *or* **sling** someone **a deefie** is to deliberately ignore him, pretend you didn't hear what he said: 'Ah said "Hi" tae her in the Post Office but she slung us a deefie, the stuck-up cow.'

deepie *or* **deepo** A schoolkids' term, short for deep trouble: 'You'll be in deepie if the teacher sees ye doin that.'

desperate If someone says he is desperate the most common meaning is that he is in dire need of a toilet: 'Ah'm no sayin Ah'm desperate, but ma eyeballs are floatin.'

devilment Something done **for devilment** is done for the sake of mischief, usually light-hearted: 'C'mon we'll phone up a pizza for yer mammy, just for devilment.'

diddy A **diddy** is a female breast or nipple. The word is also used to mean a fool or stupid person: 'That big diddy hasny got a scooby.'

To diddy about *or* **around** is to behave stupidly or fail to act seriously: 'Chuck diddyin about wi they speakers.'

A **diddywasher** is another word for a stupid person, used mainly by schoolchildren. I imagine this comes from being regarded as fit for no more exacting task than washing a baby's dummy after it has fallen on the ground.

didgy[1] A **didgy** is a dustbin: 'Ah'm gauny fling they rollerblades in the didgy if Ah find them lyin here again!'

didgy[2] A **didgy watch** is a digital watch.

diesel A mixed drink, consisting of lager, cider and blackcurrant, served by the pint. I suppose if you don't like the taste you can always empty it into your car's fuel tank: 'Ah remember huvvin three pints a diesel. After that it's emdy's guess.'

dig up To provoke or goad someone: 'That guy's been diggin me up aw night.'

dillion (pronounced *dullyin*) A child's term for a single hard blow, often inflicted with the head: 'Big McConnell gied um a dillion.'

The word is also in wider use to mean anything exceptionally good: 'Ah'm gettin a mountain bike fur ma birthday an it's a pure dillion!'

ding A dent or bash: 'Ah see sumdy's pit a ding in yer bumper.'

dinger This word (which is pronounced to rhyme with *singer*) appears only in the phrase **to go one's dinger.** The meaning is to do something very energetically (like *go one's duster*) or to lose one's temper in a big way: 'Where've ye been tae this time? The boss's goin his dinger.'

Presumably it has something to do with a bell being rung vigorously.

dingy (pronounced *dinjie*) *or* **dinny** A schoolkids' word for the dining hall: 'Ah'll get ye at the dinny at the end a this period, right?'

dinner school One might be forgiven for thinking this was an eating academy, but it is actually a school canteen or hall (sometimes known as the **dinner hall**) where lunches are served: 'Would ye rather go to the dinner school or take pieces?'

dizny This broad Glaswegian version of *doesn't* gave rise to the well-known crack about an inefficient place of work as being 'Disneyland' (because such-and-such dizny work, so-and-so dizny work, and so on).

dizzy *or* **dissy** If you make a date with someone and then fail to turn up you are said to have given that person a **dizzy**: 'What's up son, did the lemon curd gie ye a dizzy?'

The term seems likely to be a shortening of *disappointment.*

Dizzy Corner A nickname for the traditional meeting place for dating couples at the corner of Union Street and Argyle Street (also known as **Boots' Corner**). So famous a trysting place is this, and so open to the gaze of passers-by, that anyone unlucky enough to have been given a dizzy will be obvious to all and sundry.

doaty *or* **doatery** These words describe a state of forgetfulness associated with old age: 'Just you get yer paws aff yer granda's sweeties, wee yin. Ah'm no so doaty as aw that.'

dobber A slang word for idiot: 'Ah telt ye Ah wantit decaf, ya dobber!'

dog If you **dog** school you are playing truant (also known as **doggin it**). A **dogger** is a child who is truanting. One way in which schools try to keep track of straying pupils is to issue persistent truants with a **dogger's card**, that is, a card that must be signed by the teacher in charge of each period of the child's timetable. The word is a variation of *dodge* in the sense of *avoid,* and is also seen as part of the term **soapdogger.**

dog's abuse Severe criticism or unpleasant treatment: 'Ye'll need tae get us a delivery a lager right away. Ah'm gettin dog's abuse aff the punters here.'

dokey To **give it dokey** means to put one's all into some activity, give it laldy: 'We'll need to give it dokey to get this finished the day.'

To **give** someone **dokey** is to give him a very hard time: 'Her maw gied her dokey fur gettin the wean's ears pierced.'

To **take a dokey** is to become extremely angry: 'He took a dokey when he heard he wisny invitit.'

doll An affectionate term of address for a woman or girl: 'How's it gaun, doll, all right?' An **old doll** is an elderly lady, particularly someone's mother: 'She's nicked up tae see her auld doll.'

done The threatening phrase **you're done** means you've had it, you are doomed: 'See when Ah get a haud a you, pal, you're done.'

doo In the Glasgow area, this Scots word for dove is more often applied to pigeons: 'He wis lyin there lik a shot doo.' Pigeon-keeping is a popular local pastime and the purpose-built **doocot** or **dooket** in which they are housed is a common sight on spare ground.

doobie A mild term of abuse meaning an idiot: 'Whit d'ye dae that fur, ya doobie?'

doof To **doof** someone is to punch him: 'He never says a word, just reached over an doofed him wan, the cheeky wee ratbag.'

A **doof** is a punch: 'You're askin fur a doof in the coupon an ye're gauny get it.'

doolander A powerful blow: 'What a thump he gave him: a right doolander!'

doolie Another word for an idiot: 'Never mind staunin there lik a bunch a doolies.'

doosh A slang word for the face: 'Ah wannered um right in the doosh.'

doowally A slang term meaning an idiot, someone not right in the head: 'There's me staunin oot in the rain lik a doowally an the door's open aw the time.'

This is probably related to the general British slang word *doolally*, meaning crazy, with the influence of the Scots *wally* thrown in.

dot To **dot** is to go somewhere, usually in a brisk manner: 'Ah think Ah'll maybe dot round to Suzy's for a paper.' 'We've been dottin about Shawlands all day.' The term is sometimes used to mean pouring something out: 'Pass us that milk till Ah dot some in ma coffee.'

double dunter 1. An instance of working two shifts back to back: 'The gaffer's wantin us tae dae a double dunter the morra.'
2. Any event or undertaking that consists of two parts: 'Saturday night was a double dunter – the pictures then a curry.'
3. Also known as **double dunt,** a double payment of benefit by the DSS, usually because the next day the recipient is due to sign on is a public holiday and the office will be closed: 'Wait till ye see: the tube'll blow this double dunter in a week then be after me for a tap.'

double wide A slang description applied to someone who is extremely fly or not scrupulously honest: 'That boay a theirs is double wide – inty evrythin, knows evrubdy.'

doughball A fool: 'Haw, doughball! That's the wrang queue ye're in.'

dough-heid Yet another term for a fool or idiot: 'It wis a hunner-watt bulb Ah telt ye tae get, ya dough-heid!' This is sometimes shortened to **dough**: 'There it's lyin right beside ye, ya dough.'

Dough School, the Unkindly suggesting a baking academy, this is a nickname for The Queen's College. Its former title, College of Domestic Science, gave rise to the name.

dout *or* **dowt** A local term for a cigarette-end: 'Ah hate these people that just open their car door an empty a big pile a douts in the street.'

down To **go down** means, amongst the betting community, to lose: 'Ah backed the favourite in the two-fifteen at Ayr but the donkey went down.' A losing line is also described as **down**: 'His pockets were full of lines, every one of them down.'

draw To **call it a draw** means to call it a day, give up a particular activity: 'We're gettin nowhere here. What d'ye say we call it a draw an head up the road?'

dreamy Daniel A name applied to a distracted or absent-minded person: 'Look at dreamy Daniel gawpin oot that windy. Must be love, eh?'

Drum, the A nickname for the Drumchapel area: 'There's two guys fae the Drum on ma course.' This construction with a shortening of the full name preceded by *the* is a common one used for well-known (or infamous) places or thoroughfares. Other examples include **the Mulk** and **the Nitsie.**

Dublin To **kick up Dublin** means to create a fuss, complain vociferously: 'Ma mammy's kickin up Dublin cause he disny want the wean christened.' Yet another sideswipe at the proverbial hot temper of the Irish.

dummy tit A baby's dummy, or as they are often marketed, soother or comforter. The term was immortalised in a child-hood rhyme intended to humiliate a suspected clype:
> *Tell-tale tit*
> *Yer mammy canny knit*
> *Yer daddy canny go to bed*
> *Without a dummy tit*

Some versions of this substitute an even more vindictive second line: *Yer tongue shall be split.*

The phrase **spit out one's dummy** means to lose one's temper in a big way, a graphic image of a toddler's temper tantrum: 'Ye want tae've seen um when Ah telt um the bad news. He pure spat oot his dummy!'

dump The core of an apple, left after eating the fruit: 'Can ye no fling yer dump in the bin when ye've finished?'

dumpie A soft or light blow, not seriously intended to injure: 'Whit's he greetin fur? That wis only a wee dumpie Ah gied um.'

dumps Among children, to **give** someone **his dumps** is to administer thumps on the back of a person whose birthday it is. One thump per year of age is allowed to each and every child who knows about the occasion.

dundy money A slang term for redundancy money: 'Ah say we should fight fur wur joabs. Yeez'll no be lang in runnin through yer dundy money.'

dunny A term for the area below the common stair in a tenement building. Such places are well-known for being dark and spooky: 'Ah dare ye to go doon the dunny at Halloween.'

duster Someone who is working very energetically may be said to **go his duster**: 'Ye'll need to go your duster if you're goin to get that finished the day.'

They always make me the edgyman cause Ah'm wee and fast...

WEE AND FAST

eachy peachy A slang expression meaning a fair division, equal shares: 'Two tae me, two tae you, that's each peachy, intit?'

This apparently comes from a chant in a children's game which begins 'Eachy peachy peary plum, when does your birthday come?'

easy Usually pronounced *eas-ay*, this is an interjection used to greet any happy event or piece of welcome news: 'Late licence is it? Easy! Here we go boys!'

This comes from football, where supporters of a team that is winning effortlessly will often exult in their dominance by chanting 'Easy! Easy! Easy!'

eat-the-breid A nickname, usually more affectionate than disparaging, for a person considered fond of eating: 'C'mon you an me'll have the last two snowballs before Big Eat-the-breid comes in.'

ecky A slang word for the drug *ecstasy*, or a tablet of it: 'There's a guy in the lavvy says he's got good eckies.' **Eckied** means under the influence of this drug: 'Leave her alane, she's eckied oot her brain.'

edgy A term used mainly by schoolchildren, meaning a look-out. To **keep edgy** means to keep a lookout: 'The wee man'll keep edgy till you an me have a fag.'

An **edgyman** is someone appointed to keep a lookout: 'They always make me the edgyman cause Ah'm wee an fast.'

I assume the term derives from the nervously watchful condition of the lookout, who must feel 'on edge'.

eejit An idiot: 'The daft eejit but a pie straight oot the oven an burnt aw his mooth.' A variation of this is **eejit-heid.**

eekies A term used to indicate a position of equality: 'We'll stick in a fiver each an that'll be us eekies.' 'Ye can take it or leave it; it's eekies to me.'

eggs The phrase **all his eggs have two yolks** is said of anyone who is always bragging about his possessions or achievements. A variation of this is **all his eggs are double-yolked.**

Eggy Toll A familiar name for Eglinton Toll, a busy road junction and landmark on the South Side: 'Ah says tae the driver "Wan an a hauf tae Eggy Toll" an he looks at us as if Ah'm a Martian or somethin.'

eh no? A confirmation-seeking question added to the end of a negative statement. It is roughly equivalent to 'isn't that right?' or 'will you?': 'That's no your motor there, eh no?' 'Don't be late comin back, eh no?'

E. K. Nickname and abbreviation for East Kilbride, a saving in time and materials for its graffiti-sprayers: 'Rab fae E. K.'

El D A nickname for the fortified wine Eldorado. The term sometimes also appears as **L. D.**

electric soup A familiar term for an alcoholic concoction favoured by those looking for the cheapest, strongest blast, a cocktail of red biddy and meths. The term was adopted as a name for a famous 'adult-humour comic' produced in

Glasgow from the early 80s onwards by a crew of merry funsters.

Elky A nickname for any male with the Christian name Alec. The phrase **get off your elky** means to get up and go, depart: 'It didny take that yin long tae get aff his elky.'

The full form is **get off your Elky Clark,** the last part of which is rhyming slang for mark, as in get off one's mark. This expression has been around for a while, as shown by the details of the man referred to. Alexander (Elky) Clark (1898–1956) was a famous Glasgow boxer, one in a long line of wee tough fighters.

Embra A broad Glaswegian version of Edinburgh: 'Course Ah've been tae Embra – wance.' The Duke of Edinburgh has been referred to for years as the **chooky Embra.**

emdy A truncated local version of *anybody*: 'Kin emdy get a gemme?'

enemy, the A way of referring to the time, indicating the belief that time is always against one. The most common use is in the question **how's the enemy?** meaning 'what time is it?'

eppy Short for epileptic fit, as in **take an eppy.** This phrase is also used figuratively to mean display bad temper or rage: 'Big Bawjaws'll take an eppy when he sees what wee Tony wrote on the playground.'

erm A local version of *arm*: 'Her erm's aw swole up efter that jag.'

err In broad Glaswegian this is the pronunciation of various words. These are:
air 'All of a sudden an elephant's puddin came flyin through the err.'
Ayr 'He's away tae the racin at Err.' The understanding of this pronunciation is vital to appreciating the cheeky remark often addressed to someone warming his backside at a fire 'Is that yer Ayshire bacon?' (is that yer erse ye're bakin).
there 'Err wan lyin err.'

evrubdy A local version of *everybody*: 'Chuck whingein you. It's the same fur evrubdy.'

ex *or* **exie** Schoolkids' shortenings of *excellent*: 'Ah've seen that wan. It wis pure ex!'

eyes Bloodshot eyes are described pictorially as being **sewed wi rid threid.** Another phrase meaning the same, equally graphic if a touch more robust, is **eyes like dug's baws**.

Someone who is so tired that he feels as if his eyes are beginning to cross may say **ma eyes are gaun thegither.**

A face like a Hallowéen cake...

face Glaswegians must be great aficionados of facial beauty judging by the number of ways they have of describing an unattractive face. Here are a few examples:

a face like a **bulldog chowin a wasp**

a face like a **burst couch**

a face like a **burst tomato**

a face like a **camel eatin sherbet**

a face like a **chewed** *or* **hauf-chewed caramel**

a face like a **Halloween cake**

a face like a **melted welly**

a face like a **wee hard disease**

a face like a **welder's binch** (i.e. bench)

a face like a **well-skelped arse**

a face like **it went on fire and somebody put the flames out with a shovel**

a face like **somebody sat on it before it was set/while it was still wet**

a face like **you get at Tam Shepherd's** (Glasgow's famous trick and joke shop)

Other ways you might use to say that you find someone unpleasant to look at are:

ye could chop wood wi that face

ye could roughcast waws wi that face

Someone who suffers from acne or has a good crop of spots may be said to have **a face like a dartboard**.

A depressed-looking person may be told that he has **a face like a wet Monday** or that his **face is tripping him.** If you have an air of pitifulness or look in need of tender loving care you may be described as having **a face that would get a piece at any windy.**

A face like fizz is an angry face, that of someone who is not trying to hide his displeasure: 'She just sat there with a face like fizz and never said a word to anybody.'

To **get a sore face** is to be physically assaulted: 'Ye better take yersel aff before ye get a sore face, wee boy.'

Yer face in a tinny! is a phrase used to tell someone that you do not accept what he has just told you. A *tinny* is a tin drinking mug as formerly used by schoolchildren, so perhaps this is an accusation of childishness. The phrase is often shortened to just **yer face!**

A crying child may have the remark made to him **what a face tae foley a baun.** This implies, I suppose, that only smiling faces should be seen following a band.

Off one's face and **out one's face** are slang terms meaning intoxicated by drink or drugs: 'Whit d'ye mean it wis a quiet night? When Ah met ye ye were pure aff yer face!'

To **moan the face off** a person is to pester him with continual complaints: 'Ah'm gettin fed up wi you hingin aboot moanin the face aff us.'

faimly Family: 'How's aw the faimly, okay?'

fair To **go like a fair** means to be very busy, bustling with activity: 'Ah've no had a sit-doon the day. The shoap's gaun lik a ferr.'

Fair, the Although not as universally observed as it once was, the Glasgow Fair (the last two weeks in July) is still the annual trades holiday. Most workers will have at least the first Monday (**Fair Monday**) as a holiday and many the preceding Friday (**Fair Friday**) as well. A large number of businesses and factories shut up shop for the whole fortnight and this is a traditional period for getting away from it all: 'That's me booked us up for Turkey at the Fair.'

fairies When a person is described as being **away with the fairies** this means he is distracted, absent-minded, dreaming, or just plain silly: 'If ye'd been payin attention instead of bein away wi the fairies ye'd know what to do.'

faither Father. Sometimes used to address an elderly male stranger: 'It's a steep hill this, intit faither?'

falsers An informal word for false teeth: 'No thanks, hen, Ah canny go the toaffees wi these falsers.'

fankle A state of confusion, physical or mental: 'She got herself into a right fankle tryin to work out what everybody's due.' When something is in such a condition it is **fankled**: 'That dampt cat's been playin wi ma knittin an noo it's aw fankled.'

far enough The phrase **I could see it far enough** is used when someone can't be bothered with the thing in question: 'Christmas isny the same when it's just yersels in the hoose. To be honest wi ye, Ah could see it far enough.' It is sometimes also used in reference to people: 'It's no that Ah don't like them but sometimes I could see them far enough.'

fawnty A joke term for a car that is in a poor state of repair: 'He drives a Fawnty . . . fawin tae bits!'

feart This means scared, frightened: 'The wean's feart fae that stupit dug a yours.'

feartie A disparaging term for a cowardly or nervous person: 'The watter's no even cold, ya bunch a fearties.'

fiddlers' rally The proper meaning of this is, of course, a concert of traditional music played by a massed orchestra of violins. To those who are cynical about the motives and conduct of our local government representatives it is an ironic term for a Council meeting.

filla A fellow; any male person: 'That's a nice big filla she's hingin aboot wi noo.' One's **aul filla** is one's father: 'Me an the aul filla's gaun tae the boolin.'

fine well An unusual construction meaning perfectly or quite well: 'You know fine well what Ah'm on about, so don't come it.'

Fire Brigutts A slang term for the Fire Brigade, probably an amalgamation of *brigade* and the older word for the brigade, *butts*: 'Pit that smelly aul pipe oot afore the neeburs send fur the Fire Brigutts.'

Firhill The North-Side home ground of Partick Thistle, the well-known and enthusiastically supported non-Old-Firm Glasgow football team: 'Are ye joinin the faithful at Firhill on Saturday as usual?' 'Firhill for Thrills' is a catchphrase attached to the stadium and what curmudgeon would deny that such have been witnessed there?

fit Ready to go or do something: 'Is that us fit? Right, off we go.'

five-eight A *or* **the common five-eight** is a phrase meaning the average person, someone without airs and graces: 'The likes a that's no for the common five-eight like masel.'

five-spot A five-pound note: 'Gie us that five-spot and Ah'll gie ye two back.' This is American in origin, like a fair number of Glasgow slang expressions.

fix out To organise, whether speaking of physical objects or arrangements: 'It'll take me half an hour to get these books fixed out.' 'Give me a bell next week and we'll see if we can fix out another time.'

fizzer A slang word for face: 'What's up wi *your* fizzer?' This must have some connection with *physiognomy*.

flakie To **take** *or* **throw a flakie** is to lose your temper spectacularly: 'Yer mammy's gauny throw a flakie if you've not got that room tidied when she comes back.' Some people elaborate on this and talk about a **blue flakie.**

fleein This means drunk, usually in a happy way: 'Listen tae aw that gigglin; they're fleein, the pair a them.' The term comes from the Scots version of *flying*.

flier To **take a flier** is to stumble over something and fall headlong: 'She didny see the dug lyin in the hall an took a flier ower the bliddy thing.'

flit To move house is **to flit**: 'They werny in that hoose long afore they flitted again.' An instance of moving house is called a **flitting** or **a flit.** Somone who is particularly dishevelled may have it said that he **looks like something that fell aff a flittin.**

The phrase **a Saturday flit's a short sit**, meaning if you move into a new house on a Saturday you are sure not to be in it long, reflects an old-fashioned superstition. Quite why a Saturday move should be considered unpropitious I do not know.

floaters A collective word for small samples of what you have been eating that find their way into a bottle that you take a mouthful from: 'Okay, ye can get a slug but don't gie us any a yer floaters.'

flute baun A marching band of flute or whistle players, as seen in Orange Walks and similar parades: 'Ah never peyed fur aw they music lessons jist so's you could jine a flute baun.'

fly for If it is said that someone is **fly for** another person or thing this means he or she is up to all the tricks involved in something, well able to avoid being deceived by that person: 'Him? He's no a problem if ye're fly for him.' 'Ye'll pass it the next time, now ye're fly for it.'

flyman A conman, or at least someone who cannot be trusted: 'Simple Simon met a flyman, goin to the fair.'

fly's cemetery *or* **graveyard** A flat cake, consisting of a thick layer of currants sandwiched between two pieces of pastry: 'Ah canny make up ma mind between the fly's cemetery an a wee Viennese whirl.' The idea is that the currants look like so many dead flies.

follow-follow brigade, the A collective nickname for Rangers supporters, from the chorus of one of their best-known songs.

folly *or* **foley** Local variants of follow: 'You jump in the aul boy's motor an foley us tae the airport.'

for If someone asks you in a bar 'What are you for?' this doesn't mean they are questioning your role or value in the scheme of things; it is simply a request to find out what you would like to drink. **For** is used in various ways to indicate willingness: 'She's no for havin it.' 'Ah'm for the lamb tikka.'

Fort Weetabix An irreverent nickname for the St Mungo Museum of Religion, from the Townhead building's wheat-coloured, deliberately rough-hewn stonework.

France A suggested destination for someone you would like to go away, without actually swearing at them: 'Ach, get tae France, you.' 'Away tae France oot ma road.'

frontyways On the model of *sideyways*, this means front end first: 'Try it sideyways, an if it disny go, take it frontyways.'

frozen snotter A horribly graphic term describing someone who has been out too long in cold, wet weather: 'Come away in oot the cauld instead a staunin there lik a wee frozen snotter.'

fun A local version of *found*: 'He thought he wis gettin away wi it but he wis fun oot in the end.'

gallus In Glasgow this is a general term of approval for anything considered excellent: 'Gallus waistcoat, wee man!' When applied to people it's more about attitude and includes elements of toughness, cheek, self-assurance and boldness: 'He jist stoats right inty the place as gallus as anythin.' 'Ye'd never get me gaun oot wi wan a these wee guys that think they're gallus.'

The origin of the word is *gallows* and the inference was that a person so described was liable to be (or should be) hanged. This is an example of a word's meaning ending up as the opposite of what it originally signified, like the American slang use of *bad* to mean *good*.

game *or* **gemme** These two forms are interchangeable in most instances, depending on how broad the individual's pronunciation may be. The second version is pronounced with a hard *g*, rhyming with *hem*.

The **game** *or* **gemme** is of course a game of football: 'We always go tae the gemme on a Saturday.' The phrase **out the game** comes from the sport, where it describes any player prevented by injury from playing on. In everyday life it is applied to someone who is extremely tired or helplessly drunk: 'Five pints an that was him oot the gemme.'

People who want to express their approval or to encourage someone else in a course of action may say **that's the game.** Conversely, the phrase **that's no the game** indicates disapproval.

gantry In a pub the **gantry** is the area (usually shelved) behind the bar where the spirits bottles are arranged for display and ease of use, including any bottles mounted in optics. As a collective term it covers the selection of spirits (malt whiskies in particular) offered in the pub in question: 'C'mon next door; the gantry's no so great in here.'

garden party An ironic term for a drinking session on waste ground or in a park, as attended by down-and-outs, alcoholics, or simply those with enough cash for some cheap strong wine or a couple of extra-strength lagers but no place to drink in: 'Never thought Ah'd see aul Charlie at the garden party. Must be in the grubber right enough.'

Gaspipe, the A familiar name for Garscube Road, running between Cowcaddens and Maryhill: 'Whit buses go up the Gaspipe noo, sonny?'

gate To **give** someone **the gate** is to sack him; similarly, to **get the gate** is to be sacked: 'They wereny long in giein you the gate oota there.'

gaun Go on: 'Gaun doon tae the chippy an get us a pakora supper.' The word is often used to tell someone to go away: 'Ah'm fed up lookin at ye. Beat it! Gaun!' On the other hand, the phrase **gaun yersel** is intended to encourage someone in what he is doing or to show approval: 'Gaun yersel, Da! You tell the wee bampot.' This probably comes from a football fan's cry in support of a player performing some individual magic.

Gaun can also mean going: 'We're aw gaun on wur summer hoalidays.'

gauny Literally this means going to: 'You're gauny get yer backside skelpt.' When part of a request or question it means are you going to, but the idea is really a firm suggestion rather than a tentative query: 'Gauny see's ower that screwdriver?' 'Gauny shut yer face, you?'

One step further, **gauny no** introduces a request not to do something: 'Gauny no keep bumpin inty us, pal?'

gear The phrase **a bit of gear** refers to a sexually attractive woman: 'Ah widny mind gettin a grip a his big sister . . . a fine bit a gear.'

geggie One's mouth: 'Why don't you just shut yer geggie an no show yer ignorance?' This is sometimes shortened to **gegg**: 'Ah might as well keep ma gegg tight shut as try tae talk sense tae you.'

Formerly, a **penny geggie** was an individual show at a travelling fair. Perhaps the idea of shutting one's geggie is related to closing the curtain on such a stall.

gemme See **game.**

gemmy Pronounced with a hard *g*, this is a term of approval meaning plucky or flash: 'D'ye think it's gemmy tae shout an swerr at yer maw?'

A youth who is seen as gemmy may be called a **gemme kid.**

gen up A phrase used to confirm or question the truth of another statement: 'We're gettin a rise next month.' 'Gen up?' 'Aye, gen up.'

Gers, the One of the nicknames of Glasgow Rangers F. C.

get Used locally to mean escort or accompany: 'If ye're goin to the shops we'll get ye along the road.'

It can also mean meet: 'Ah'll get ye ootside The Horseshoe at half-six.'

gettin The use of this to mean *becoming* is fairly standard. What is different about Glasgow usage is that this verb is often found at the end of the sentence: 'They're kinna snobby gettin.' That is, they're becoming somewhat snobbish.

ginger Any carbonated soft drink may be called **ginger,** often contained in a **ginger boatle**: 'Cola's the only ginger left.' Perhaps this is a hangover from an earlier time when ginger beer was the only fizzy soft drink available.

Singin ginger is a picturesque term for alcoholic drink, reflecting pithily the predisposition towards song of the well-refreshed: 'Listen tae that racket. They've been at the singin ginger again.'

On meeting a red-headed girl a patter-merchant might say **Hello, Ginger, are ye still fizzin?** This is a double play on words, using ginger in the soft-drink sense as well as the nickname.

The phrase **bother your ginger** means to make an effort, show some interest, and is usually found in the negative: 'See that promotion she got? That could've been you, but you wouldn't bother your ginger.'

gingy (pronounced *jinjy*) A ginger bottle: 'Sumdy wapped us oan the nut wi a gingy.'

gink (pronounced with a hard *g*) A slang word meaning to smell unpleasantly, or an unpleasant smell: 'These denims a mine are ginkin.' 'There's some gink in that changin room.'

girth A fat belly, usually of the type produced by devotion to beer: 'Your aul boy's got some girth on him since he retired.'

give To **give** someone **into trouble** means to give someone a row or land someone in trouble: 'The teacher gave me into trouble for giggling.'

glabber This means mud or dirt and is a variation of the more general Scots word *clabber*. 'He slipped in the lane an got his troosers aw glabber.'

glass cheque A jocular piece of slang for a drinks bottle that has a deposit on it and can be used in lieu of cash when returned to a vendor: 'Here, son, this glass cheque's yours if ye run oot tae the ice-cream man.'

Glesga *or* **Glesca** Broad Glaswegian versions of the city's name. Other variations do occur, such as 'Glasgie' or 'Glasgae' but these are not native to Glasgow, coming instead from other regions of Scotland or from off-target English attempts at a Glasgow accent.

Glesga grin A slang term for a slash on the face: 'Let's see what the Cockney wide boy looks like wi a Glesga grin.'

Glesga nod A slang term for a head-butt: 'Never mind arguin wi the diddy – gie um the Glesga nod.' This is also known as the **Glesga kiss.**

globe Used locally to mean a light bulb: 'That's no another globe went, is it?'

go A **go** can mean a fight: 'What's *your* problem, pal? Want yer go?' The phrase **a square go** means a one-to-one fight, unarmed, this being regarded as a fair way to settle a confrontation: 'They think because you come from Glasgow you inevitably end an argument with the offer of a square go.'

   To go can mean to feel like or be in the mood for: 'Could ye go another sandwich, minister?' It is also used in the sense of handle or tolerate: 'Ah canny go the whisky at aw. It gies me the boke.' 'She's nice but Ah canny go that man a hers.' It can also mean to have the skill or ability to guide and control some kind of vehicle: 'It took him years to learn to go a bike.' Another use is the sense of being able to speak or understand a language: 'Can ye not go the Gaelic at all?'

go-bi-the-waw Literally go-by-the-wall, this is a disparaging name applied to a slow-moving or lackadaisical person: 'We'll miss that train if big go-bi-the-waw disny get a jildy on.'

gommy[1] To call someone **a gommy** is to call him an idiot: 'No that wan, ya gommy; *that* wan.' Someone or something considered stupid-looking can be labelled **gommy** or **gommy-lookin**: 'Ye tryin tae tell us that gommy-lookin big dreep's the gaffer?'

gommy² A local version of *gammy*, i.e. artificial, false, as in **a gommy leg**; or counterfeit, fake, as in **gommy money.**

good This occurs in various local constructions. The **good room** of a house is the room kept for entertaining visitors, containing the best furniture and decor, and not used day to day: 'Ah've telt ye before ye're no tae play in yer Granny's good room.'

Someone who is described as taking **a good drink** is considered a regular heavy drinker: 'She used tae take a good drink but she's aff it noo.'

If an activity is done **good style** this means it is done in an admirable or energetic way: 'We were getting through the carry-oot good style.' 'They're gettin on good style wi the decoratin.'

Similarly, to do something **like a good yin** is to do it enthusiastically: 'The wee soul's gettin stuck in like a good yin.'

Gorbalonian A native of the Gorbals: 'It was a mixed marriage . . . he was a Govanite and she was a Gorbalonian.'

go through To **go through** a person is to tell him off in no uncertain manner: 'When their faither heard what they'd been daein he didny hauf go through them.'

Gourock This town on the firth of Clyde features in the proverbial phrase **away to one side like Gourock**, which means lop-sided, unbalanced, skew-whiff: 'Come here till I fix your hat. It's away to one side like Gourock.' This seemingly derives from the fact that Gourock is built mainly on one side of a hill.

Govan This world-famous district of south-west Glasgow has long since made its mark on the dialect.

Good God in Govan is an exclamation or mild oath, invented no doubt for the sake of the alliteration rather than the likelihood of the burgh's being chosen as the location for the Second Coming.

Sunny Govan is a nickname for the place, used mainly by the inhabitants, that typifies the Glasgow blend of love of your own patch tempered with ironic realisation of its shortcomings.

What's that got to do with the price of Spam in Govan? is another of these elaborate ways of asking, What's this got to do with the subject? How is that relevant?

A *or* **the Govan kiss** is a slang term for a head-butt: 'He says he walked inty a door but Ah seen um gettin a Govan kiss ootside the chippie.'

Govanite The term for a native of Govan: 'Ma uncle Joe's the secretary of the Sydney Govanites Association.'

gowpin *or* **goupin** This means extremely painful, as if throbbing: 'Ma erms're gowpin wi humphin aw they messages.' 'That's me aff the bevvy. Ma heid's been gowpin aw mornin!'

granda One's **granda** is one's grandfather: 'Say cheerio tae yer granda, boys.' Another form of this is **granpaw.**

granma One's grandmother: 'Some a ma granweans cry me Granma and wi some a them Ah get Nana.' **Granmaw** is another version.

granny To say **your granny!** in response to someone else's statement is to imply that he is talking nonsense. It occurs in fuller forms, used to precisely ridicule the other person's claim, as in: 'Ma big brother's a brain surgeon.' 'Aye, yer granny's a brain surgeon.' The most popular catchphrases along these lines are 'Aye, an yer granny was a cowboy' and 'Yer granny on a scooter.'

It could be said, though, that in these days when many pensioners live longer and more active lives the idea of Granmaw knocking out the odd prefrontal lobotomy, roping a longhorn, or burning rubber is no longer so ludicrous.

grave-nudger A slang term for someone perceived as being a little too long in the tooth: 'You should stick tae the over-30s nights alang wi aw the other grave-nudgers.'

greaser A slang word for a lump of spittle and mucus hawked up from the back of the throat and spat out: 'Some clatty article's gobbed a big greaser oan this windy.'

Green Lady A familiar term for a health visitor, originally from the colour of the uniform. Although nowadays they no longer wear a uniform this is still the term in general use: 'She's friendly wi Mrs Sloan, ye know, her that's daughter's a Green Lady.'

greet Someone who **greets** is crying. An episode of this may be called **a greet**: 'Just have a right good greet an ye'll feel better.' If someone is feeling less than sympathetic to a person who is crying he may say: 'The more ye greet the less ye'll pee.'

Parents often warn arguing children that they are heading for a **greetin match**, meaning that both or all parties in the dispute will end up in tears.

A **greetin face** is a face that looks as if its owner has a complaint on his mind or is about to burst out crying: 'Och, what's up wi yer aul greetin face noo?' Anyone who wears such an expression habitually may be called **greetin-faced**: 'Ye canny have a laugh wi that greetin-faced git.'

grey van A vehicle in which, according to folklore, people recognised as insane are transported to a place of secure accommodation: 'If ye carry on lik this it'll be the big grey van that comes for ye.'

The colour of this legendary conveyance sometimes varies from place to place and can be blue or green.

grip If a person is described as having **a good grip of Scotland** this means that they have exceptionally large feet.

The phrase **get one's grip** means to have sexual intercourse: 'He filled her up wi drink so he'd be sure tae get his grip, an here it wis him that flaked oot.'

To **get a grip** of someone is to lay hand on him or her, with a view to embracing, cuddling, and if fortunate even further liberties: 'Check him in the Crombie. Ah widny mind gettin a grip a him.'

If a person needs to be told to calm down or keep the head, he may be advised to **catch a grip, come to grips,** or, with that extra edge of condescension, **get a grip of your liberty bodice.**

grog A local version of *spit*: 'Chuck yer groggin, will ye?' 'There's a big grog on the pavement.'

grot or **grotbag** A slang term for an unpleasant or dirty person: 'Get yer paws aff us, ya mockit wee grotbag!'

This comes from the widely used British slang word *grotty*, meaning horrible, dirty, unattractive etc.

grousebeater A slang word for an alcoholic down-and-out: 'There's always grousebeaters hingin aboot that wee arcade.'

growler A **growler** is any person who seems surly or bad-tempered: 'Oor new English teacher's a right growler.' In the plural **growlers** are sausages: 'You shove on the growlers while I butter these rolls.'

grun The ground: 'Wait till yer maw sees ye rollin on the grun in yer good claes.'

gub One's **gub** is one's mouth: 'Ah wisht Ah hudny opened ma gub.' **To gub** a person is to give him a punch in the mouth. The verb can also mean to defeat convincingly: 'They'll get gubbed when they come to Parkhead.' An instance of this may be called a **gubbing**: 'We took a gubbin after you were sent off.'

guidie A school term for a guidance teacher: 'Miss, are you gauny be ma guidie next year?'

gums To **bump your gums** is to speak, especially nonsensically: usually used when rudely asking someone to refrain from doing it: 'If you wid stoap bumpin yer gums fur wan minute Ah'd tell ye whit we're gauny dae.'

The insulting part is of course the suggestion that you are toothless and presumably senile.

gun To **gun** something is to use it up quickly, or, particularly in the case of drink, to swallow it rapidly: 'See that retsina? The only way to drink the stuff is to gun it right back.'

guttered Another word meaning drunk: 'The last time I went out with them I ended up guttered.' This probably derives from the idea of a person being so drunk that he falls over and has to lie in a gutter.

gutties A popular name for any variety of rubber-soled soft shoes, especially sandshoes: 'If ye've got gym today mind an take yer gutties tae school wi ye.' This comes from *gutta-percha*, a form of rubber used to make such soles.

guy The use of **guy** to mean any male person is much more prevalent in Glasgow than in most other parts of the UK, another illustration of the city's enduring identification with and love for all things American (particularly movies): 'At wee guy stays up ma close.'

. Away an run up ma humph .

hackit An unflattering description, meaning ugly, that seems to be more often applied to women than men: 'That yin fancies hersel an she's pure hackit an aw.'

haddie This Scots word for *haddock* is often used to mean a foolish person: 'Hurry up an take that photie. Ah'm staunin here posin lik a haddie.'

hair ile Hair oil, a predecessor of today's hair gel, used as a euphemism for *hell*: 'Whit the hair ile are ye rantin on aboot?'

hairy A **wee hairy** is an abusive name for a young woman considered sluttish: 'The only ones that go to that club are neds and wee hairies.'

To **take a hairy fit** (sometimes shortened to **take a hairy**) means to go crazy with anger: 'Your brother'll take a hairy when he sees the state you've got his Armani jacket inty.'

half *or* **hauf** A single measure of spirits, most commonly of whisky. In pubs the size of a **half** can vary, depending on whether a bar serves a quarter-gill measure or something smaller. In less formal surroundings, such as a person's home, the size of the measure is totally arbitrary: 'He knows how to pour a good half, your old man.'

Many older pub drinkers will order **a half and a half-pint**, meaning a whisky accompanied by a half-pint of beer, usually heavy.

halfers *or* **haufers** When two individuals agree to buy something between them, sharing the price equally, this is to **go halfers** *or* **haufers**: 'Ah'll go halfers wi ye on a new video.'

Hallaleen A local variant of *Halloween*: 'When Ah saw the get-up she wis gaun oot in Ah thought it must be Hallaleen.'

hallelujah **The Hallelujahs** is a nickname for The Salvation Army. Someone who joins this organisation may be said to **go hallelujah**: 'She an her mother went hallelujah after the faither died.'

Hameldaeme Literally, home will do me, this is used as a mythical holiday destination, especially by people who can't afford to go anywhere: 'If Ah get paid aff it'll need tae be Hameldaeme for us this summer.'

hammer Various phrases are connected with this humble tool. If you want someone else to stop doing something or turn something off you might ask them to **give it the hammer**: 'If there's nobody watchin that garbage give it the hammer for goodness' sake.'

To **put the hammer on** a person is to ask him for a loan of money: 'Ah'm gettin scunnered wi him pittin the hammer oan us every Saturday night.'

The hammer's on means that there is trouble on the way or that strict measures are to be enforced: 'The hammer's on just now, so keep your head down for a bit.'

A fine figure of a woman may be described as being **well hammered thegither.**

Hampden *or* **Hampden Park** Located on the South Side of Glasgow, this is the national stadium for the Scottish football team and also the home ground of Queen's Park F. C.: 'We're on our way to Hampden, we shall not be moved!' **The Hampden Roar** is the famous noise of the crowd at international or Cup games.

handbaw or **haunbaw** This means to lift or carry a heavy load by hand rather than mechanical means: 'Never mind waitin on a forklift. The three ae us'll handbaw this.'

This is probably another import from football, where *handball* is the deliberate illegal use of the hands by any player other than a goalkeeper to play the ball.

handers or **hauners** A friend, particularly one who helps out in a fight, is often known as **a hander**: 'Tell yer handers tae keep oot the road an Ah'll gie ye a square go.' To shout for **handers** in a fight is to summon friends to pitch in and help.

To hander someone is to help in this way: 'C'moan an hander us, wan a yeez!'

hang¹ or **hing** To **hang** or **hing wan on** a person is to give him a punch: 'On yer way before Ah hing wan on ye.' **To hang someone's jaw aff his face** is to slash him severely: 'If Ah get you Ah'm gauny hang yer jaw aff yer face, ya wee crawbag.'

See also words beginning **hing-**.

hang² A common euphemism for *hell*: 'Whit the hang's gaun on here?' 'Ach, tae hang wi the lot a yeez!' 'That's a hang ae a thing, is it no?'

hanks In broad Glaswegian this is a version of *thanks*: 'Hanks a million, pal.' This is one of several examples of pronunciations in which a *th* sound becomes *h*.

happy day A mixed drink, consisting of a wee heavy (bottle of strong ale) poured into a pint glass which is then topped up with draught heavy: 'Gie's a pint a heavy, barman ... naw, make it a happy day. Ah could do wi wan.'

Happy Larry A proverbially cheery person whose name is ironically applied to any glum individual or killjoy: 'We were aw havin a great laugh till Happy Larry came hame.'

hard-hearted Hannah A jocular name applied to any woman who is relatively strict in her dealings, definitely not a soft touch: 'It's no use askin hard-hearted Hannah for the mornin off just because your budgie died.'

Apparently this comes from a popular old song about 'Hard-hearted Hannah, the vamp of Savannah.'

hardman A man who is or wants to seem violent and tough: 'He thinks he's a bit of a hardman but you could kick lumps out of him.'

haud The phrase **haudin up the bar** is a jocular way of describing someone who is leaning on the bar in a pub, as if he was indeed holding it up instead of the other way round: 'Ah might a known the perr a yous wid be in here haudin up the bar.'

hauf-scooped A slang term meaning somewhat intoxicated, rather than completely helpless: 'On yer bike, you. Ye're no turnin up hauf-scooped tae take me oot.'

haun-knittit Literally hand-knitted, this is used to describe anything that looks ill-made, especially home-made: 'Ah know ma garden-sprinkler looks kinna haun-knittit, but at least it works.'

haw A term used to call for the attention of someone else: 'Haw, Jim! Where's the stop for the fifty-nine bus?'

Hawkheid A familiar name for Hawkhead Hospital, a psychiatric establishment near Paisley: 'Ye'll need tae stoap worryin yersel or it's Hawkheid ye'll end up.'

head *or* **heid** To head is to leave, depart: 'If ye're wantin a lift Ah'm headin in five minutes.'

To put *or* **stick the heid on** someone is to head-butt him: 'Mad Boab went an stuck the heid oan the bouncer.'

Keep the head *or* **heid** is a phrase used in advising someone to calm down. Some people elaborate this into **keep the heid an Ah'll buy ye a bunnet.**

One way of saying that you are suffering with a hangover is **Ah've got a heid lik a sterrheid,** the idea being that your head

71

is pounding as if it was a common landing in a tenement close that endures the tramp of many heavy feet.

There are various phrases containing **head** *or* **heid** used in telling someone that he is daft or scatterbrained. These include: **yer heid's fulla mince, yer heid's fulla broken bottles, yer heid's fulla magic snowballs** (whatever they are), **yer heid's fulla wee motors.** My personal favourite in this line is **yer heid's fulla dominoes an they're aw chappin** which not only implies that your head is filled with these items but that none of them is any use.

You might also say **yer heid's up the lum** or, if you prefer to be more offensive, **yer heid's up yer own arse.**

One of the dismissive phrases in popular use is **away an bile yer heid.**

A graphic if unlikely threat is to tell someone he will **get his head in his hands (to play with)**: 'You'll get your head in your hands to play with if you don't finish that homework for tomorrow.'

If you say of someone (even yourself) **the heid's away** or **the heid's went** this means the person so described has become absent-minded or stupid. It can also mean a person has become vain.

headbanger *or* **heidbanger** A slang term, predating the sense of a heavy-metal fan who tosses his head from side to side in time with the beat, meaning a crazy person: 'There's no way Ah'm gauny argue the toss wi that heidbanger.'

This is sometimes shortened to **header** *or* **heider.** The only explanation for the term that occurs to me is that it suggests the person in question is mad enough to bang his own head against a wall.

heard it! A sarcastic response to any statement or claim that you find hard to believe, the inference being that this is like an old joke that you have heard before: 'That's the first time I've ever been sick through drink.' 'Aye, heard it!'

heart-roastit Someone who claims to be this means that he or she has become exasperated, worried, or angered by someone or something, especially if the annoyance has been going on for some time: 'Him an his two daft brothers've got their poor mammy heart-roastit wi their fightin an gettin inty bother.'

heave, the **The heave** is what you give to a person or thing you no longer want. This covers such acts as sacking an employee, jilting a lover, ejecting a person from a premises, and throwing out unwanted items: 'Ah see JD's bird gave him the heave.'

heavy dunt, the Like **the heave**, this is given to someone or something you want rid of or to something that you want to stop: 'If he had any sense he would give that caper the heavy dunt.'

heavy team, the A collective term for a group of tough individuals, especially a gang. It is often used jocularly to refer to any bunch of people who are supposedly frightening or in authority: 'We better get back to our desks: that's the heavy team coming out of their meeting.'

heedrum hodrum A disparaging label for traditional Gaelic music and song: 'He says he canny go the heedrum hodrum stuff on the telly but Ah like tae watch the laddies dancin in their kilts.'

The term comes from the ignorant non-Gaels' attempt to reproduce in words the sound such music supposedly makes. There's a joke connected with the term that involves a punchline along the lines of: 'You get a haud ae um an Ah'll heider um.'

hee-haw Nothing to do with donkeys, this is a term (meaning *nothing at all*) used by people who prefer not to say the much stronger two-syllable version that has the same final sound: 'There's hee-haw use you tryin tae get that motor tae start.'

heidie A **heidie** is a school headmaster: 'Ah seen her waitin ootside the heidie's oaffice.'

It can also mean a header at football: 'The wee man scored wi a divin heidie.'

To heidie something, usually a football, is to strike it with one's head: 'Imagine that tube tryin an overheid kick when he could've heidied it in nae bother.'

Heidies *or* **headers** is an informal type of football game in which the emphasis is on heading the ball. **Wee heidies** is a name applied to this when played in a close or other similarly restricted space, or can mean simply one person continually heading a ball against a wall as a means of improving his heading ability or just to pass the time.

heidnipper Someone who nips your heid, i.e. scolds you, or harps on about something: 'His aul doll wis such a heidnipper he shot the craw tae London just tae get away fae her.'

heid-the-baw A nickname that can be applied to almost anyone. More often than not it is used affectionately, but it can take on a suggestion of contempt: 'Ah thought Big Heid-the-baw would be here by now.' 'Ye'll get no sense oot a that shower a heid-the-baws!'

Obviously this comes from football but why someone who heads the ball, rather than kicking it, should be so patronised I do not know, unless the suggestion is that too many impacts of ball with head affect the brain.

hems To stop a person doing something or to control his behaviour is to **put the hems on** him: 'His folks'll soon put the hems on him when they come back their holidays.' The phrase originally meant putting a collar on a working horse. The meaning has been extended to cover making something impossible: 'If Ah've tae work late that'll pit the hems on gaun tae the pictures the night.'

hen A friendly term of address for any female, whether known to the speaker or a stranger: 'Yer wean's flung away his dummy, hen.'

Her, Him Many people refer to their husband or wife not by their given names but by the anonymous pronoun. I use capital letters to show that there is never any doubt as to which particular person is the subject of the discussion: 'Ah just came oot tae get Him somethin fur His dinner.' 'That's me bought the weans their Christmas presents. Ah'll just need tae get somethin for Her noo.'

here Used as a shortened version of *here is* or *here are*. 'Here Wee Joey on the phone.' 'Here wan here.'

het When children are playing tig, the one whose task it is to chase the others is **het**: 'Tracy says Ah'm het but she never touched me.' This is a particular use of the Scots word for *hot*.

hey-you A slang term for a coarsely-spoken or insolent person: 'Ah'm no too happy wi that crowd she's in wi at school. That wan she brought hame the day wis a right wee hey-you.'
   This comes from the use of 'hey you' by such people as the opening remark in a conversation with a stranger.

hielan A Scots word for *Highland*, used to mean illogical, naive, or clumsy: 'Ah'll show ye how tae dae the thing right, no that hielan way you're gaun aboot it.' A male native of the Highlands may be referred to as a **Hielanman**: 'Ye canny take the breeks aff a Hielanman.'

Hielanman's Umbrella, the The stretch of Argyle Street covered by the Central Station railway bridge gained this nick-name when it was a well-known meeting place (conveniently sheltered from rain) for Highland emigrants living in Glasgow: 'Ye need tae go alang tae the Hielanman's Umbrella tae get that bus.'

high heid yin A fairly irreverent term for anyone considered powerful or in a position of authority: 'Wasn't he one of the high heid yins in Strathclyde Region at one time?'

hing[1] An equivalent of *hang*. 'She's loast that much weight the claes are hingin aff her.'
   The phrase **hing as it grows** (with *grows* pronounced to rhyme with cows) is used when something is to be left alone because nothing useful can or should be done: 'Ah've done ma bit. Noo it'll just need tae hing as it grows.' The image seems to be of fruit left to develop naturally on a tree.

hing² In broad Glaswegian *thing* is pronounced like this: 'Ye know the kinna hing Ah'm oan aboot?' When **hing** forms part of another word like *something, everything, nothing, anything* the final *g* joins the initial *t* in disappearing altogether: **somehin, everyhin, nuhin, anyhin**.

hing aboot wi A typically unromantic Glasgow expression meaning to go out with, have as one's boyfriend or girlfriend: 'Who ye hingin aboot wi since ye elbowed that geek oot the bank?'

hing aff This means get off, let go of me: 'Never mind yer wee cuddle, ya ignorant pig, just hing aff, wull ye?'

hingie A traditional activity in tenement buildings, to **have a hingie** is to lean out of an open window in a flat and pass the time of day by watching the comings and goings in the street, occasionally conversing with passers-by or occupants of other open windows.

hingin thegither Literally, hanging together, this is a conventional, somewhat downbeat, reply to someone who asks how you are doing. The implication is that things are okay, but no better than that. It can act as a question to someone who might be considered to be under pressure: 'How're ye the day, young yin . . . hingin thegither?'

hingmy *or* **hingwy** In broad Glaswegian this is a variant of **thingmy**: 'Away an ask hingmy if he'll gie ye a len a that whit-d'ye-cry-it.'

hing oot One way of saying that you are very tired is **ma eyes are hingin oot ma heid**.
   A **hing-oot** is an insulting slang term for a woman of easy virtue: 'Aye, she's no bad lookin . . . for a clatty wee hing-oot.'

hingy *or* **hingin** A graphic term applied to someone who, while perhaps not actually ill, isn't feeling very well: 'She's no hersel, the wee soul, she's been hingy aw week.'

hink A local version of *think*: 'Whit d'ye hink a Scotland's chances oan Saturday?'

hit To **have a hit for yourself** is to think highly of yourself: 'That boss a yours has got a real hit for himself, hasn't he?'

If someone is likely to forcibly reject something you might offer it may be said that he will **hit you with it**: 'Nae use giein her Gancia if she wants champagne. She'd hit ye with it.'

hoachin This can mean infested with, full of: 'The back garden's hoachin wi wasps.' It can also mean extremely busy, full of people: 'Ye canny get a seat in there on a Saturday night; it's always hoachin.'

hoachy This has the same sense as *jammy*; that is, very lucky, often in a way that is considered undeserved: 'We played them aff the park for nearly ninety minutes then they went an got a hoachy goal.'

holiday giro This is a slang term meaning a double payment of benefit because of a public holiday, and can be used to mean any unexpected bonus.

Home Ekies Short for Home Economics, a school subject: 'Mammy! Daddy wullny eat the sausage roll Ah made um in Home Ekies!'

homer[1] A job done by a tradesman in his own time, as opposed to one done as part of his regular employment: 'Ah'll get that done for ye cheaper than that. Ah know a wee sparkie that does homers.'

homer[2] A football referee who is considered to be favouring the home team during a match: 'No way was that a penalty! That ref's a homer.'

honey A desirable member of the opposite sex: 'C'mon you an me'll go to the jiggin an get aff wi a couple a big honeys!'

Conversely, someone considered lacking in physical beauty may be described as **no honey**: 'That yin thinks he's God's gift, an he's no honey either.'

honk To **honk** is to throw up: 'He spent the hale trip honkin ower the side.'

A honk is an instance of this: 'Ye'll feel better after a good honk.' **Honk** is vomit: 'Ma shoes are aw splashed wi honk.'

honkin A term used to describe anything considered very smelly or simply of poor quality: 'The last party a theirs Ah went tae was pure honkin.'

hooch Pronounced with the *ch* as in *loch*, this is the exuberant cry uttered by people engaging in Highland dancing or by those looking on: 'With a chorus of hoochs they got stuck into the Gay Gordons.'

hook To punch, with one hard blow: 'Ah'm no carin how hard he's meant tae be. If he disny shut it Ah'm gauny hook um.'

hooley A term that came to Glasgow from Ireland, meaning a boisterous social occasion such as a noisy house party: 'Man, there's some hooley gaun on up the stair the night.'

hoor's knickers A disparaging term for Austrian blinds, a silky-looking ruched form of curtains.
   The phrase **up and doon like a hoor's knickers** is used to describe anything that fluctuates: 'The price a petrol's gaun up an doon lik a hoor's knickers the noo.'

hooverin up The practice of going round at a party or other convivial occasion swallowing any unfinished drinks that seem to be unwanted: 'He wis daein a bit a hooverin up an he took a big swally oot a can that had a fag-end in it.'

horse in *or* **get horsed in** To set about something enthusiastically. This can apply, for example, to a job of work, but it is most commonly used in relation to food, perhaps with the sense of eating like a horse: 'Horse inty they pies. Kid on ye're at yer auntie's.'

horse's oranges A jocular term for horse-droppings: 'If he spies horse's oranges lyin in the road he's out like a shot to snaffle them for his garden.'

hot-pea special A portion of marrowfat peas in vinegar; a traditional cafe delicacy beloved by, among others, the immortal Francie and Josie.

how Used locally to mean *why*: 'How're ye no comin?' With the addition of *no* this becomes *why not*: 'She's no gaun.' 'How no?' Some people elaborate this a little further into **how fur no?**

howlin A slang term meaning very smelly: 'His boots were howlin so Ah slung them oot in the close.'

howpin Another smelly word: 'Ah'll need tae clean oot that fridge. There's somethin howpin in there.'

how's it gaun? Literally, how's it going, this phrase is used as a greeting: 'Hiya Charlie, how's it gaun, ma man?'

huckle To **huckle** a person is to grab hold of him and physically move him from one place to another. This can mean being thrown out: 'Me 'n' Tam had tae huckle the bampot out before he startit a fight.' It can also mean forcing someone inside: 'The polis started hucklin guys inty their van.'

hudgie To **catch** *or* **take a hudgie** is to hang onto the back of a moving vehicle, an activity indulged in by reckless children: 'He wis catchin a hudgie oan the back ae a bin lorry an he fell aff an goat hut wi a guy oan a mountain bike.'

Huggy Loch *or* **Huggy** A familiar name for Hogganfield Loch, in the East End: 'He tried tae let on he wis an experienced sailor when aw he'd sailt wis an oary boat on Huggy.'

hughie *or* **huey** To **hughie** is to vomit: 'That guy looks lik he's gauny hughie in a minute.' 'Ah think Ah've got that disease where ye stuff yer face then have a right good huey.'

The full version of this is **hughie bush**, showing even more plainly that the words are intended to represent the sound of vomiting.

hullo! A cry of celebration at some welcome event: 'Hey, Ah think the rain's went aff. Hullo! We're away noo!'

hum-a-ding-dong A slang term meaning very smelly: 'Man that cheese is pure hum-a-ding-dong!'

humph To **humph** something is to carry it, usually something heavy or awkward: 'Some hotel this! Ye've tae humph yer ain cases up tae yer room.'

A humph is a hump in one's back: 'She'll be gettin a humph carryin that wean aboot aw the time.' The word is used in the phrase of rude dismissal **away an run up ma humph**. Another phrase in which it appears is **would that no sicken yer humph?** meaning, isn't that disappointing or disgusting. If you are asked to explain your behaviour and find that you have no better excuse than it simply occurred to you, you might say **it just came up ma humph**.

A **humphy** or **humphy-backit** person is someone with a hunchback.

humphy-tumphy A mother's pet name or endearment for a child: 'Who's Mammy's wee humphy-tumphy then?'

Hun A nickname for a Protestant, particularly a Rangers supporter, which is sometimes applied to the Rangers team: 'If the Huns get bate the day the Bhoys'll be top of the table.'

hunner A hundred: 'There's hunners an thoosans a midgies oot there.'

hunt To hurry someone away from a place: 'Ye get nae drinkin-up time in there. They start huntin ye right efter the bell.'

It can also mean to get rid of an undesirable person, run him out of town: 'Don't talk tae me aboot cooncillors – they should be huntit, the hale jing-bang o them!'

hurl This means a ride in or on a vehicle: 'They're away a wee hurl in the new motor.' A stingy person may have it said of him that he is **aye looking for a free hurl**.

hurtit Someone who gets **hurtit** is injured: 'Was emdy hurtit in that crash?'

hut A local version of *hit* (past tense): 'He hut us furst, Miss!'

huv, hud Local variants of *have* and *had*: 'Youse've no hud tae pit up wi whit Ah've hud tae, neither yeez huv.'

huvtae *or* **huvtae case** A slang term for a wedding made necessary by a pregnancy, i.e. they 'have to' get married: 'It wis a dead quiet weddin . . . well, what can ye expect fur a huvtae case?'

He grabs a big dod a Irish Steak, slaps it between two ootsiders an says "That'll need tae dae us till Ah get somethin tae eat"

Ibrox _or_ **Ibrox Park** The home ground of Rangers F. C.: 'His faither stopped gaun tae the gemme efter the Ibrox Disaster in seventy-wan.'

icey _or_ **icie** Short for ice-cream van: 'That tune sounds dead like the one the icey plays.'

Idleonian A rather old-fashioned term for someone who is out of work, particularly if it is suspected that this condition has been chosen rather than imposed. It is also extended to mean anyone who seems lazy or is not pulling his weight: 'Oh aye, here am Ah knockin ma pan in an youse Idleonians can sit an read yer papers.'

ile This Scots version of _oil_ turns up in the phrase **away for ile**, applied to anything that is worn out, exhausted, or non-functioning: 'Ma aul legs're away fur ile, son!'

indescribables A nickname for pakora: 'Ah'll have a double portion of yer indescribables an gie's plenty sauce, eh Jim?'

inky A school term, used by pupils and teachers alike, for a felt-tip pen: 'Away and ask Mr Mackay for a packet of inkies and come right back here with them . . . and don't run!'

intit no? This literally means 'isn't it not?' and is a common double negative, frequently used by a speaker seeking confirmation of some negative statement: 'It's nae use gaun up north in this weather, intit no?'

into *or* **inty** Various local phrases make use of this term. If you say you are into something this means that you are willing to have it or take part in it: 'Ah'm inty the lamb masala this time.'

If someone tells you he is **inty your heid** this means he intends to physically assault you. A person wishing to encourage someone else to come to blows with a third party may say **inty his heid!** This can be jocular, of course, particularly when a fuller version **inty his heid wi a teaspoon** is used, making the comparison with smashing in the top of a hard-boiled egg.

Similarly, a football fan may exhort his heroes to greater commitment in tackling the other side by crying **get inty them!**

Irish Steak A jocular nickname, presumably a dig at Irish poverty, for cheese: 'He grabs a big dod a the Irish Steak, slaps it between two outsiders an says "That'll need tae dae us till Ah get somethin tae eat."'

*Aw naw, here's a jam sandwich
at ma back*

jag A **jag** is an instance of being pricked by something, especially
an injection: 'Ah hate it when the dentist gies ye a jag in the
mooth.' **To jag** is to prick: 'She jagged her finger on the barbed
wire.' 'Put yer shoes on – somethin on the grass might jag
yer foot.'

To **jag up** is a drug-users' term for injecting oneself with a
narcotic.

Something that is **jaggy** is sharp-pointed (like a jaggy bit of
glass) or prickly (like a jaggy nettle).

Jags, the A nickname, punning on the second part of their
official title, for Partick Thistle F. C.: 'Of course the guy's a
romantic. He's a Jags fan, isn't he?'

jaiket *or* **jaisket** A jacket. To **haud the jaikets** means to be in
attendance at some event without taking part, be an onlooker:
'Don't ask me what's gaun on, pal. Ah'm only haudin the
jaikets here.' This comes from the ceremony of a playground
fight in which the two combatants have their square go while

a supposedly neutral third party takes custody of their jackets and any other restrictive accoutrements.

If someone's **jaiket's on a shoogly nail** this means that his position is not secure, that there is a threat of losing his job. The literal meaning is, of course, that the nail on which the person is accustomed to hang his jacket has become loose and the next time the person tries to hang up the said jacket it may, along with the nail, fall to the floor: 'Late again, eh? You better screw the nut, sonny boy, cause yer jaiket's on a shoogly nail.'

jake A slang term for methylated spirits (as drunk by alcoholic down-and-outs) or red biddy: 'His guts must be rotten wi aw that jake he pours doon his thrapple.'

Jaked up means drunk, and **jaked out** means unconscious through drunkenness. Both terms have overtones of contempt as they imply that the individuals so described are winos: 'It's a wee bit rough an ready, this boozer. Ye'll maybe see wan or two guys jaked oot at a table.'

jakey A slang word for a down-and-out, especially one who obviously drinks lots of *jake*: 'This aul jakey comes up an bites ma ear fur the price of a cup a tea.'

jammy dodger A proprietory brand of biscuit, consisting of two round pieces with jam in between. In the dialect this term is borrowed to mean someone considered very lucky: 'Big Dave won a motor in a raffle, the jammy dodger!'

jam sandwich A jocular term for a police car, from the Strathclyde force's livery of white with a central red stripe along the length of each side: 'Aw naw, here's a jam sandwich at ma back.'

janny A janitor in a school: 'Here comes the janny wi his bucket a sawdust.'

jarred up Another expression meaning drunk, i.e. having swallowed a few jars (pints): 'It's stupit gettin jarred up before the gemme. Ye miss hauf ae it trailin back an forth tae the bog.'

jaup A small amount of spilt liquid, a splash: 'They've left wee jaups of emulsion on the windy pane.'

jaur A glass jar: 'Ye'll get a brass screw in that jeely jaur ower there.'

jawbox A rather old-fashioned term for a sink. The *jaw* part is a Scots word meaning to pour, and the *box* probably comes from the fact that, especially in tenement flats, sinks were often boxed in to give cupboard space below them.

jeely Jam or jelly (the preserve rather than the pudding). A **jeely piece** is a jam sandwich and a **jeely jaur** is a jamjar.

Jeely-eater A nickname for an inhabitant of the Vale of Leven, deriving from the time when Irish navvies constructing the Forth and Clyde Canal lived in this area and were said to be too poor to eat more than jeely pieces every day.

jeez-oh A mild oath, obviously a euphemism for *Jesus*: 'Jeez-oh, neebur, whit'll we dae noo?' A similar exclamation is **Jesus Johnnie!** I have no idea who the Johnnie might be or how he got dragged into it.

jersey The phrase **sell the jerseys** (sometimes **jumpers**) means to sell out, betray your cause. The origin of this is, of course, football. Any team, but particularly a national side, that plays disappointingly and doesn't seem to want to try very hard, may be accused by disgruntled fans of having sold the jerseys. In everyday life the phrase may be heard in contexts where someone is representing others: 'I would just like to remind the chairman that he and the other officials are meant to be goin in to negotiate, no sell the jerseys.'

jiggin, the Any kind of organised dance, not necessarily involving jigs: 'Ma Maw likes gaun tae the jiggin at The Plaza.'

jile A local version of *jail*: 'He should get the jile fur that, so he should.'

jimmies *or* **gymmies** A schoolkids' term for gymshoes or plimsolls: 'Ach, Maw, these jimmies are gettin too wee fur us.'

Jimmy *or* **Jim** A name used to address any male stranger in a friendly manner: 'What time's the next train, Jimmy?' 'Hey, Jim, is that emdy's seat?'

Jimmy Johnstone When waiting at a pedestrian crossing in Glasgow and the light indicates that you may cross, you might hear someone say: 'C'mon, here's Jimmy Johnstone.' After all, I suppose the small-statured former Celtic player is the nearest thing in life to a wee green man.

jiner A local version of *joiner*. 'He calls hissel a jiner but he never served his time.' This comes from the pronunciation of *join* as *jine*. 'Ah think Ah'll jine the Ermy.'

jinkies To say that something is **the (wee) jinkies** is to describe it as excellent: 'Aye, yer granny's trifle's the wee jinkies, intit, son?'

jobby The act or product of defecation; also used as a term for an unpleasant individual: 'That guy can be a right wee jobby at times.' It can also be a verb: 'See if Ah get a haud a that cat that jobbies on ma flower bed . . .'

joggies *or* **joggy bottoms** The trousers of a jogging suit, popular as informal wear: 'Ma teacher says Ah've no tae wear ma joggies tae school.'

joiner A pejorative name applied to someone who joins a company drinking in a pub, partakes of several rounds, then disappears before taking a turn to buy: 'Aye aye, here Wullie the Joiner comin in. Tell um it's his shout an see whit he does.'

jooks A slang term for trousers: 'Aw c'moan, tell that stupit dug a yours no tae jump up oan the good jooks, eh?'

jorrie A glass marble. A game of **jorries** is a game of marbles. This is probably connected with *jaur*, meaning a glass jar. Someone who is said to talk with **a jorrie in his mouth** is seen as speaking poshly or affectedly.

jotters To **get** *or* **be given your jotters** is to be dismissed from your employment: 'If it was up to me the whole lot of ye would be gettin yer jotters for this.'

juke If you put something **up your juke** you put it, for conceal-ment or protection, under the front of your outer clothing: 'Here's the teacher comin! Shove that book up yer juke!'

jump If a person associates with a particular individual or group he may be said to **jump aboot** with them: 'Is that the guy that jumps aboot wi Mad Boab an aw them?'

Jumpin is a vivid term meaning extremely angry: 'Say nothin tae yer Daddy; he's jumpin aboot this.'

If a person decides to join in a fight that has already started he is said to **jump in**: 'It serves ye right. Naebdy asked you tae jump in.'

Jungle, the An affectionate name for the formerly terraced stand at Celtic Park, dominated by the team's most vociferous supporters: 'The massed choirs of the Jungle were already celebrating before the final whistle.' Perhaps because of this, Celtic fans are sometimes referred to as **junglies**, although this may equally come from the rhyming slang **Jungle Jim.**

just Like **but** this often appears at the end of a statement, in this case meaning to imply moderation or shortness of time: 'Take wan each just.' 'Ah'll be ready in two shakes just.'

jye A local pronunciation of the letter *J*. It is able to exist side by side with the standard *jay*, which it does not replace in such common combinations as *DJ*, *OJ*, *PJs*, etc.

Poor Hughie's gaun aboot like a hauf-shut knife since that wee wife o' his done a bunk...

KB Shorthand for **knockback**: 'Ah hear the boyfriend gave ye the big KB.'

keech Rhyming with *dreich*, this is a term for any kind of filth, but especially excrement: 'Mind yer feet on that dug's keech.' Like other similar words this can be used to mean a disliked person: 'What's that wee keech sayin noo?' **Keechy** is used to describe anything that is filthy or has been dirtied by excrement: 'Sumdy's left a keechy nappy in that bin.'

keekaboo A local name for the game of peekaboo as played to amuse very young children.

keeker A black eye: 'That's a right keeker ye've got.'

keelie Glaswegians are often referred to as **keelies**. Some regard this as an insult, given that the word originally meant a low-class disreputable person; others adopt the label with pride, but many see it as morally neutral: 'I really don't know what she's thinking of, bringing a keelie like that to the house.' 'Ah'm a Glesga keelie, born an bred!'

The Highland Light Infantry, a former British Army regiment recruited mainly from Glasgow, was nicknamed **the Glesca Keelies.**

keepie-uppie To play **keepie-uppie** with a football is to juggle the ball, never letting it touch the ground, using any part of the body except the hands and arms: 'Mind Slim Jim playin keepie-uppie wi it at Wembley in sixty-seven?'

kegs A slang term for men's underwear: 'These kegs are stranglin us.'

Kelvinside The archetypal posh area of Glasgow's West End lends its name to the type of refined accent (in which, for example, *sex* is what you buy coal in) that often comes across as affected: 'Mai, mai, we're being awfully Kelvinsaide, aren't we?'

kettlebelly A disrespectful name for anyone with a fat stomach: 'Go easy on the pizza or ye'll end up like kettlebelly here.'

keys The cry of **keys!** *or* **keysies!**, usually accompanied by a double thumbs-up which is known as having one's **keys up**, is used in children's games when a player wants to call a truce or gain temporary immunity from any punishment that is going. Some adults make ironic use of this when they feel they are being unduly pressurised or berated: 'I was giving him a piece of my mind when he shouted "Keys!" and I couldn't help laughing.'

Khyber Pass Another nickname for Gibson Street (see **Curry Alley**): 'We'll dodge down the Khyber Pass an grab a pint in the Doublet.'

kick Someone who **kicks with the left foot** is a Roman Catholic (also known as a **left-footer**). Someone who **kicks with the wrong foot** is a person regarded in some circumstances as professing the wrong religion: 'There's nae use tryin tae get a job wi them if ye kick wi the wrang fit.' Oddly enough, there seems to be no equivalent expression about kicking with the right foot. Apparently the saying comes from the idea originating in Northern Ireland that a man digging who uses his left foot to dig the spade in will be a Catholic and the man who uses his right will be a Protestant.

kicking A term used to mean a sound battering: 'They told him he was on a kickin if he ever went back there.'

kilt A local variant of *killed*: 'A guy up oor close kilt hissel.'

kin A local variant of *can*: 'Kin you no shut up for a minute?' 'Ye kin whistle fur it.' The negative of this is **kin't**: 'Ye kin jist get yer ain, kin't ye?' Sometimes a double negative appears, using both *kin't* and *no*: 'Ah kin make ma ain dinner, kin't Ah no, Mammy?'

kinna A form of *kind of*: 'Kinna stupit-lookin, in't he?' 'What kinna motor's she got noo?'

kipper's knickers, the A local equivalent to the bee's knees, i.e. something wonderful: 'That yin thinks she's the kipper's knickers since Big Joe got aff wi her.'

knacked Like *knackered*, of which this is perhaps a contraction, this can mean very tired, broken-down, unserviceable: 'We no near finished yet? We're aw knacked.' 'It's no the tape, it's your video that's knacked.'

knife To describe someone as going about **like a half-shut knife** means that he looks depressed or introspective: 'Poor Hughie's gaun aboot lik a hauf-shut knife since that daft wee wife a his done a bunk.'

The expression obviously arises from the image of a sad person walking bent over, looking at the ground, compared to a pen-knife with its blade neither fully opened nor properly closed into the handle.

knock To **knock** something is to steal it: 'Who's knocked ma pieces?' Someone who steals is a **knocker**: 'Gie's that ruler back, ya wee knocker.'

knock back To **knock** something **back** is to turn it down or reject it: 'The management upped the offer to three per cent but the union still knocked it back.' This rejection can happen to people as well as things: 'Ah said Ah'd gie her a lift hame but she knocked us back.'

An instance of either of these is a **knockback**: 'Ah hear she applied for that job an got a knockback.' 'Cheer up, son, never had a knockback aff a lassie before?'

knot If you are laughing enthusiastically you may be described as **knottin yourself**: 'Ah wis knottin masel when the aul man startit tellin us his daft stories.'

K. P. An abbreviation and nickname for the Kinning Park area of the South Side: 'Jeanie, here a couple from the K. P. that knew your mother.'

The pair a them wis lummed up before they even got tae the reception.

laldy An odd word, meaning punishment or enthusiastic participation. To **give it laldy** means to give one's utmost enthusiasm and effort to whatever it is one is doing: 'The boy wi the Lambeg drum wasny hauf gie in it laldy.' To **give someone laldy** is to give the person a severe chastisement, whether physically or verbally: 'Aye, yer granda used tae gie us laldy wi a slipper for the likes a that.'

Lally's Palais *or* **the Lally Palais** A nickname for the Royal Concert Hall, at the head of Buchanan Street, from its being planned and built while Pat Lally (later Lord Provost) was head of the City Council.

lamp To **lamp** someone is to hit him: 'He just walked up tae the big diddy an lampt him right in the mooth.' It can also mean to throw something: 'That's the guy that lamped a hauf-brick at the polis.'

Lanny A nickname for Lanliq, a proprietary brand of inexpensive fortified wine: 'Gie um a boatle a Lanny an that'll be him happy.'

lavvy A toilet, shortened from *lavatory*: 'Aw naw! Ma wallies've went doon the lavvy pan!'

A plumber is sometimes referred to disrespectfully as a **lavvy-diver**: 'Ah'm no puttin ma haun doon there. That's a joab fur a lavvy-diver.'

lay it off To talk about something at great length and with an air of imparting vital information: 'Ah wish she wid stoap layin it aff tae us aboot gaun tae Uni.'

leader-off The person who takes the lead in an activity, whether it be in an innocent pastime like singing, or as the leader of a gang: 'I might have known you'd be the leader-off in this carry-on.'

left-footer *or* **left fitter** A slang word for a Catholic: 'They're aw left-fitters in that department.'

lemon top A pint of beer with a little lemonade poured into it, not enough to make it a shandy but enough to give it a slightly more refreshing taste to a particularly thirsty customer: 'See's two lagers, hen, an make mines a lemon top.'

lend *or* **len** A loan: 'See's a len a yer ladders, will ye?' To **take a len** *or* **loan** of a person is to exploit him without him knowing it, often in a manner that makes him look gullible and credulous: 'Ye'd think he'd learn a lesson seein the right len o him she took the last time.'

length To **go the length of** means to travel as far as: 'We're no gaun the length o Paisley but we could drap ye at The Haufway.'

Light Blues, the A nickname for Rangers F. C., from the colour of their jerseys.

like that The phrase **I was** (she was, we were, etc.) **like that** often crops up in a conversational narration meaning the speaker was surprised, shocked, dumbfounded etc., depending on the context. Obviously it is meant to be accompanied by a pantomime of the relevant facial expression or bodily stance, but it is commonly used without any such visual aid and can be described as mere verbal padding: 'She says "You're no comin wae us" an Ah wis lik that. Ah says "How've Ah no tae get?" an she wis lik that, an she says . . .'

line A **line** *or* **bookie's line** is a betting slip, or the actual bet: 'Ah'll maybe nip down an put a wee line on.' 'This line's beat.' 'He says he's left the line in his ither jaiket.'

A **line,** also known as a **sick line** *or* **doctor's line,** can be a certificate from a GP attesting to a sick employee's unfitness for work: 'Yer self-certificate's ran oot. Ye'll need tae get a line fae the doctor.'

Some shops or stores operate a discount facility for staff, and a person to whom this is available is often said to have **a line for** that particular store: 'Her next door's got a line for Marks.'

Lipton's orphan A proverbial poor-looking person: 'Ah tried on your coat but it wis far too big fur us. Ah looked like Lipton's orphan in it.' Originally Lipton's Orphan was an advertising name applied to a pig, as sold by the famous grocer Thomas Lipton. It somehow became fixed in the proverb as if it was an actual, human orphan.

Lisbon Lions, the The nickname for the famous Celtic F. C. side who, in Lisbon in 1967, became the first British team to win the European Cup: 'Sure Wee Jinky wis wan o the Lisbon Lions, Da?'

live up with A common phrase meaning to live in sin, cohabit with someone to whom you are not married: 'Aye, that's him that left his wife an weans tae live up wi some floozy fae Partick.'

loaded A descriptive term meaning full of the cold, having a runny nose, sore head etc: 'Aw ya poor soul, ye're loaded. Away hame tae yer bed wi a hot toddy.'

Lodge, the Sometimes pronounced *ludge*, only one lodge is understood by this, i.e. the Orange Lodge: 'Whit d'ye make a that referee . . . another wan up for the Lodge, eh?'

'lok Nickname for Pollok F. C., a well-supported Junior side based at Newlandsfield on the South Side: ''lok hopes dashed in penalty shootout.'

long The expression **as long** means an unspecified but lengthy time: 'Her wean's photie wis in that photographer's shop windy for as long.' **Long enough** similarly means a long period: 'If he makes a baws ae it this time he'll wait long enough for another chance.'

The phrase **a long road for a short cut** is used when what is intended to be a quicker route to travel or a faster way of doing something seems to take longer than the usual way: 'I know it looks like a long road for a short cut but it works out quicker in the end.'

look The unusual construction **get your head looked** is a local way of referring to a psychiatric examination: 'Ye said naw tae an offer lik that? You need tae get yer heid looked, pal!'

loop *or* **loop-de-loop** A crazy person: 'Ah canny believe you're hingin aboot wi a loop like that.'

loosie A slang word for a cigarette sold individually in a shop, as bought by those who are short of funds or under age: 'This guy'll sell ye a loosie nae bother, on ye go.'

Lorne sausage Sausage meat shaped into oblong blocks before being cut into slices: 'Away roon tae the butcher's for a half pun a Lorne sausage and a couple a slices a beef ham.' Also known as **square sausage**.

loss This is often used as a verb meaning *to lose*: 'Ah'm gauny loss the heid if this cairries oan!'

loupin From a Scots word for *jump*, this is used to mean extremely painful: 'Ah bet yer heid's loupin efter last night.'

It can also mean infested (as in 'Look at that wean clawin her heid. She must be loupin.') or very busy with, full of: 'The toon's loupin wi Welsh rugby supporters.'

low-flyer A nickname for a measure of The Famous Grouse, a popular proprietary brand of whisky (from the behaviour of the bird).

luckies A nicely apt word for things of value found in rubbish bins, as hunted by midgie-rakers: 'Ah went doon wi the rubbish an fun an aul dosser gaun through the bins for luckies.'

lucky bag A bag containing sweets and a cheap toy or gift, as bought by children from sweetie shops. The point is that the purchaser doesn't know exactly what is in the bag until it is opened, and the term is often used to disparage something the speaker doesn't think much of: 'That's some portable phone ye've got; get it in a lucky bag, did ye?'

lucky middens A slang term for bins where substantial *luckies* are likely to be found. Also extended to describe an area where such middens are the norm: 'I hear you've moved to Newton Mearns; that's you up in the lucky middens now, eh?'

lumber **To get a lumber** is to meet and establish a relationship with a member of the opposite sex: 'How'd ye get on at that party . . . did ye get a lumber?'

To lumber a person is to chat her or him up successfully: 'That guy you're hingin aboot wi wis tryin tae lumber us last night.'

lummed up A slang term for drunk: 'The pair a them wis lummed up before they even got tae the reception.'

Lum, of course, is a Scots word for chimney, but apart from seeing someone as reeking with the fumes of alcohol the connection between drunkenness and chimneys escapes me.

lumps To **kick lumps out of** someone is to give him a good hiding: 'It does give one a poor impression of a hostelry when one enters the lounge to find two of the clientele kicking lumps out of one another.'

The image of his meat . . .

ma¹ My: 'Ma maw's a millionaire!'

ma², mammy, maw All of these are used locally to mean *mother*. 'Couldny be better, Ma!' 'Ye canny shove yer Granny, cause she's yer Mammy's Mammy . . .' 'Haw, Maw! Whit's fur ma tea?'

Many Glaswegians are peculiarly sensitive to insults to their mothers (apparently it's okay to slag fathers), and this has given rise to such barbs as **yer maw's a big man, yer maw's a brickie, yer mammy's a bun** and so on.

Maccy, the A nickname for Maxwell Park, a public park on the South Side: 'We had a shot on a pedal boat on the Maccy pond.'

At one time it was said that you were not a fully-fledged Kinning Parker until you had fallen into Maxwell Park pond while hunting for baggies.

MacWhachle **Wee MacWhachle** is an affectionate name for a toddler: 'Wait till ye see Wee MacWhachle comin over when Ah crumple this bag a sweeties.'

maddy A crazy person: 'He was shoutin an bawlin like a maddy.'

Someone who exhibits violent anger may be said to **take a maddy**: 'The parkie'll take a pure maddy if he catches ye pickin they flooers.'

mad skull A local term for an unstable or wild person: 'The way that bam drives he should have a sticker in his back windy sayin "Mad Skull On Board".'

malky A cutting or stabbing weapon, especially (and originally) a cut-throat razor. To **get the malky** is to be physically attacked: 'You're gauny get the malky if ye don't get aff yer mark.'

To **malky** a person is to attack him, especially using a bladed weapon: 'Tell the crapbag Big Ronnie's on his way roon tae malky him.'

To **get malkied in** is to do something with great vigour and enthusiasm.

The term seems to have originated as the first half of a piece of Glasgow rhyming slang: Malky (short for Malcolm) Fraser meaning *razor*. My researches have failed to unearth the Malcolm Fraser thus commemorated.

mark To scar, used as a threat: 'Get oot ma road afore Ah mark ye.'

masel Myself: 'Ah'm a fool tae masel, so Ah am.'

mate aboot To associate with someone as friends, have a particular person as your best pal: 'Yer faither an me used tae mate aboot thegither when we were in John Brown's yard.'

meat Used in the sense of food in general (not just cooked animals) this turns up in the phrase **it's your meat that makes ye bonny**. It is often said of a child that is plump and healthy, well-fed-looking, that he is **the image of his meat**.

mee-maws A nickname for the police, imitating the sound of a squad car's siren: 'Ah got wakened up in the middle of the night wi the mee-maws fleein doon the street.'

There's the old joke about the proud mother who has three strapping sons in the police force. Towards the end of their dinner she asks 'Who's for merr puddin?' and hears in reply 'Me Maw, me Maw, me Maw!'

melt To **melt** a person is to strike him powerfully: 'He jumped ower the table an meltit him wan.' This comes from the earlier Scots use of the term to mean to hit someone in the region of the *melt* or spleen.

The phrase **get inty his melt** is used to encourage another person to attack a third party or, if a fight is already in progress, to put more effort into it: 'Are you gauny take that crap aff the likes a him? Get inty his melt!'

mental To **go mental** is to lose your temper in a big way: 'She'll go pure mental when she sees that phone bill.' Another version of this is to **throw a mental**.

Someone who is wild, unstable, or given to extravagant losses of temper may be called a **mental** *or* **mental case**: 'A gang a mentals got on the bus an widny pey their ferr.'

Mentalness is the state of being crazy or a display of this: 'What's gaun on in there the day is nothin but pure mentalness.'

mentions When a youth is scrawling graffiti on a wall or other surface and one of his mates wants to be named in the roll of honour he will be told 'Gie's mentions.'

This is sometimes shortened to **mensh** or **menshies**: 'How'd you no gie me an Hammy menshies?'

mere A local form of *come here*, shortened in speech from the already compressed *c'mere*. 'Mere you! Whit's this you're sayin aboot me?'

merrit Married: 'She's merrit ontae wan a they McLaffertys fae Smith Street.'

mess To **mess** is to interfere, to get involved with someone else's business, especially in way likely to cause a fight (whether intentionally or not): 'Are you messin wi me, pal?' 'Ye don't mess wi the best.'

Someone who causes trouble in this way (or anyone who simply makes a mess) may be called a **messer**: 'That wee messer's just stirrin it.'

message To **go (for)** *or* **do the messages** means to do the shopping. The items bought are known as **messages**: 'Wis that you Ah saw staggerin up the road wi a ton a messages?' A shopping bag is often referred to as a **message bag**. Any kind of errand, not just to buy something, may be called **a message**: 'She'll be back in a minute: she's just away a wee message.'

To **give someone the message** is to convince him of the error of his ways, either by verbal chastisement or physical force: 'Boy, Ah'll gie you the message all right if Ah catch ye at this wee gemme again.'

messin A mildly abusive name, particularly used for naughty children: 'He's et the hale packet, the greedy wee messin!' The word originally meant a small dog.

mibby Maybe: 'That'll mibby teach her a lesson.'

Mick's blood A slang term for Guinness.

midden This can mean a dustbin or the area behind a tenement block where the dustbins are kept. It is also applied to places or people considered slovenly or unclean: 'The dirty aul midden hasny had a bath for months.' 'Get this midden of a room tidied up right now.'

midgie Another word for **midden**: 'There's a deid cat lyin in the midgie.' A **midgie-bin** is a dustbin, which is liable to be emptied by a **midgie-man** (dustman), into the back of a **midgie-motor** (bin lorry).

Someone who, for one reason or another, searches rubbish bins for things of value or use may be called a **midgie-raker**.

Milk *or* **Mulk, the** A familiar name for the Castlemilk area in the south of the city: 'We're meetin up wi a couple a boys fae The Mulk.' In recognition of this a local paper is called *The Milk Round.*

millions A substantial quantity (rather than number) of anything: 'He flung that can in the bin an there was millions left in it!'

mince For some reason the name of this traditional filling for pies or accompaniment for totties has been borrowed by the dialect for a variety of meanings.

It can mean nonsense or deliberate untruthfulness: 'That's pure mince you're talkin.' 'Do they expect us to believe this mince?' Another meaning is anything nasty or dirty: 'What's this mince on the sleeve of ma coat?'

It is taken as a measure of density, whether of the brain or another substance: 'The guy's as thick as mince.' Some people refer to a pint of Guinness as a **pint of mince**. A person who seems very quiet or downcast may be told they are **sittin there like a pun a mince**.

To **sicken someone's mince** is to spoil something for him or deflate him: 'It didny half sicken his mince when he didny get that bonus.'

minder A small gift, often bought as a thank-you token for someone who has done you a kindness: 'She's been a right good neighbour over the years. I'll need to get her a wee minder before we go.'

mines A variation of *mine*: 'He's already et his dinner an now he's wantin mines!'

ming Anything that smells unpleasant may be said **to ming**: 'That cheese disny half ming.' **A ming** is a stink: 'See the ming when Ah took the lid aff the bin?'

Mingin means unpleasantly smelly but its use is extended to cover anything that is considered bad: 'Ah wis that lookin forward tae that film an it wis pure mingin.'

minted A slang term used to describe anything you approve of or think is excellent: 'Ah hear ye passed yer test. That's

101

minted, wee man.' Perhaps this derives from the idea of a brand new shiny coin, newly minted, that stands out from the other dull coins in your change.

It is also used to mean wealthy: 'Have ye seen their motor? They must be pure minted.'

miraculous (usually pronounced *marockyoolus*) This means extremely drunk. It has been around a long time, as shown by this 1873 extract from the former Glasgow periodical *The Bailie*, in which a court witness was asked to describe the degree of drunkenness exhibited by an accused person: 'I've seen him the waur o' whusky; he had got a dram, an' was a little intoxicated, but he wasna miraklous.'

The term is sometimes shortened to **maroc**: 'Did ye see her last night? Maroc or what?'

miss To **miss yourself** is not to somehow become aware of the absence of your body, but to fail to experience something enjoyable through not being in the right place at the right time: 'Ye missed yersel no comin on Saturday . . . it wis a right good night.'

If you are angry with someone and are telling a third party exactly what you will do when you catch the offender, you might say **Ah'll no miss him** or, in its fuller form, **Ah'll no miss him an hit the waw**.

mix Someone who deliberately sets out to cause trouble between two other parties may be said to **put the mix in**: 'Never mind what the wee ratbag says, he's just tryin to put the mix in.' An alternative version of this is **the mixy**.

moan A shortened form of *c'moan*, come on: 'Are ye comin or no? Moan then!'

mobbed Crowded with people: 'Ye couldny get near the shops. They were aw mobbed.'

mockit *or* **mawkit** This can mean soiled or dirty: 'Ye're no gaun oot in they mockit troosers, are ye?' It is also used to mean dirty in the sense of obscene or lewd: 'How come ye never actually see anybody takin oot wan a they mawkit videos?'

model A hostel or lodging-house for single homeless people: 'Ye're gaun aboot lik somethin oot a model.' **A modeller** in this case is someone who lives in a model. The term comes from the more formal Model Lodging House, the original title of many such establishments.

mollocate To beat up or thrash: 'The aul man'll mollocate you if he gets ye.'

Monday Book A common nickname for a book of DSS benefit vouchers, so called because the vouchers are all dated to be payable on Mondays: 'The wean wis playin wi ma Monday Book an noo Ah'm gaun mental lookin fur it.'

monty A slang expression meaning hurry up or don't be silly: 'Where is that eejit? Here, you, monty!' This is a shortening of one or two similar phrases, the least offensive being **monty grips**, which literally means come to grips.

moolly A term used to describe someone considered mean or miserly: 'The moolly aul get never gied us a bung.'

moony A slang word for a slow embracing dance, or the music for it, most commonly observed at the end of a disco when the romantic tracks are played: 'Ah'm that shy Ah hide in the lavvy when a moony comes oan.'

moose's meat A nickname, fairly contemptuous, for cheese: 'Ah could never be a vegetarian. Ah need merr tae keep me gaun than moose's meat an rabbit fodder.'

mooth The mouth. Somone considered to be well-endowed in this department may have it said of him that he has **a mooth like the Clyde Tunnel**. A person who has irregular or stained teeth may be described as having **a mooth like a row of condemned hooses** _or_ **buildings**.

One of the unpleasant after-effects of a heavy drinking session, especially when mixed with smoking, is **a mooth like a pocketful a douts**. A similar expression is **a mooth lik a badger's bum** _or_ **arse.** One can't help but wonder why a badger should be considered particularly unpleasant in this department and, indeed, how anyone found out.

A moothful a heidies is what is suffered by someone who is head-butted: 'You wantin a moothful a heidies, pal?' Another version of this is **a moothful a dandruff**.

The phrase **you've a mooth** indicates an offer of food or drink to a guest: 'D'ye know, Ah sat in that hoose fur a good hoor an a hauf an they never thought tae say "ye've a mooth"!'

moothie A mouth-organ or harmonica: 'Her aul boy's a dab hand at the moothie.'

morra, the A local version of *the morrow*, that is, tomorrow: 'Ah'll be away the day, the night, an the morra.' **The morra night** is tomorrow night: 'It's no oan the night, it's the morra night.'

mortalled Another word for drunk, a local variant of the Scots term *mortal*: 'He tries tae tell us he only hud wan or two. Away, Ah says, mortalled wisny in it!'

Mount, the A familiar name for the Mount Florida area on the South Side: 'Ah liked it when we stayed up in the Mount. It wis a real wee community.'

movin Moving, a descriptive adjective meaning infested with lice: 'Ah'd tae sit next tae this poor wee soul at the doactor's. Nae jaiket nor nothin, an his heid wis movin.'

Muldoon's picnic A term used when a miscellaneous group of people sit down to a disorganised meal: 'I wouldn't exactly call it a dinner party. It was more like Muldoon's picnic.'

Sampson was a stroongman,
he lived on fish an chips.
He went along the Gallowgate
pickin up the nips

-nae *or* **-ny** Literally meaning *not*, this is a negative suffix common enough in Scots, as in *willny, cannae*, etc. It is used on its own by local children to contradict the last thing said to them, as if adding the negative to a word the speaker has used: 'Right, you're comin hame this minute.' '-Nae!' 'Ye are so!' '-Nae!' This kind of argument is not only maddening but invincible if persisted with, as there is nothing you can say that can't be thus negated. You either give up or resort to nonverbal measures.

naebdy *or* **noabdy** Two local variants of *nobody*: 'Naebdy came tae the door.' 'Is there noabdy wantin spiced onions?'

nae nae kiddin Definitely no kidding, an emphatic insistence that you are telling the truth, used especially by children. It can also be a question, meaning you're not having me on, are you?: 'Look, Ah'll definitely get ye in for nothin.' 'Nae nae kiddin?' 'Nae nae kiddin.'

naw A local variant of *no*: 'Aw naw, ma galluses've snapped!'

neb Another word for *nose*: 'Just you keep yer aul neb out a this.' It is also used to mean a nosey (or sometimes cheeky) individual: 'What was that wee neb askin ye?' **A neb** can also be an instance of being nosey or prying: 'Is she no back from the toilet yet? She must be havin a neb round upstairs.'

To neb is to pry into other people's business, be inquisitive: 'Tell him to mind his own business instead of comin round here nebbin.'

neck To **get** *or* **take a red neck** is to be embarrassed to the point of blushing: 'Ah get a red neck every time that wean opens his mouth.'

In a bar, if a customer asks for a bottle of beer **by the neck** this means he doesn't want it poured into a glass, whether because he intends to use a glass he already has or because he means to drink straight from the bottle: 'Gie's two pints a seventy an a Sol by the neck.'

To **go on one's neck** means to fall heavily, especially flat on one's back: 'She walked onty the wet flerr an went on her neck, the soul.'

ned A hooligan or criminal, usually young, or someone who acts or looks like one: 'I'm fed up getting cheek from these neds that loiter outside the chip shop.' Sometimes used as an adjective: 'This is pure ned behaviour.' 'He's got a right ned face on him.'

neebur A **neebur** is a neighbour, and can also mean specifically a person who works beside or with you: 'Yer uncle was ma neebur in Butters years ago.' The word often appears as a term of address to someone you feel friendly towards: 'How ye gettin on, neebur? Hingin thegither?' **Neebs** is a shortened form of this: 'All right, neebs?'

needle To **take the needle** is to take offence: 'We were just muckin aboot. There wis nae need fur him tae take the needle.'

neither Used in forming additional reinforcing statements at the end of a negative remark, as in: 'He'll no be away aw day, neither he will.' The opposite of this is **so**.

newp When decimal currency was introduced in the early 1970s everything was counted in new pence, which was typically and immediately shortened to **newps.** Although no longer in common everyday use you will still hear the word in certain fixed contexts, such as a twenty-pence piece being called **twenty newps**: 'Any a youse goat twenty newps fur this parkin meter?'

new start An employee who has only recently joined a firm, often the butt of wicked japes: 'Right, whit wan a youse comedians sent the new start fur a tin a tartan paint?'

nick To **nick** is to go somewhere quickly or briefly: 'He's nicked oot for a fag.' The phrase **nick about** has several meanings. It can mean to circulate in a particular area: 'He's always nickin about the shoppin centre on a Saturday.' It is also used to refer to someone who has an active social life and is often seen around and about places of entertainment: 'She fairly nicks about, that yin.' To **nick about with** means to frequent the company of: 'He's just a guy Ah nick aboot wi.'

nineteen-canteen An imaginary date long ago, time immemorial: 'Ah've no been doon the watter since nineteen-canteen!'

nip To **nip** is to be sore: 'Gie's an aspreen or somethin . . . .ma heid's nippin.' It can also mean to hurt: 'These new shoes are nippin ma feet.' To **nip someone's heid** is to perpetually nag or upbraid him: 'Ah'm fed up wi you nippin ma heid aboot that washin machine.'

To **nip** a person can mean to pick him or her up, to meet and establish a relationship with him or her: 'Ah'm gaun oot tae see if Ah can nip a wee burd the night.' 'Hey, you! Ma pal says she wants tae nip you.'

The expression is also used to mean to borrow money: 'Ah'll see if Ah can nip the brother for a ten-spot.' Someone who is trying to secure such a loan is described as being **at the nip**: 'Kid on ye don't see um. He'll be at the nip, sure as guns.' A person who is always borrowing money may find that he is labelled by this habit: 'Don't tell us ye lent a fiver tae Jimmy the Nip!'

To nip a cigarette is to put it out by pinching the lit end, usually with a view to smoking the remainder later on: 'It startit rainin, so Ah'd tae nip ma fag an stick it behind ma ear.'

A nip can be a partly-smoked cigarette that has been pinched out in this way or simply a cigarette-end thrown away, as commemorated in the following delightful rhyme:

Samson was a strongman,
He lived on fish an chips.
He went along the Gallowgate
Pickin up the nips.

nippie A brief or quick excursion: 'Well do a wee nippie inty the bookie's on the way back.'

nippy sweetie The original meaning of this is a boiled sweet that has a sour flavour or makes the mouth feel hot. It is most commonly used now to mean a drink of spirits: 'Ah've no got time for a pint, but if ye put ma arm up ma back Ah'll mibby manage a quick nippy sweetie.'

It can also mean a person with a short temper or sour disposition: 'He can be a bit of a nippy sweetie if ye rub him up the wrong way but he's no a bad guy really.'

Nitsie, the A nickname for Nitshill, a housing scheme in the South Side: 'It's gauny be some night ... the boys fae the Nitsie are aw comin.'

Noddytown A nickname for Cumbernauld, partly from the *-nauld* part of the 'new' town's name and partly because it doesn't seem like a 'real' town to many Glaswegians. So, next time they ask you what it's called, you'll know.

noise To **noise** someone **up** is to deliberately provoke or irritate them: 'Dae Ah get the impression you're noisin me up, shorty?'

This seems to have originated as a motoring term meaning to sit behind another car at a traffic light, revving your engine in an intimidatory manner.

Nollie, the A local nickname for the Forth and Clyde Canal, which passes through the north of the city: 'Ah huvny hud so much fun since Ah used tae go tae the ferret-racin on the Nollie banks.'

This comes from a shortening of a local pronunciation of canal, i.e. *ca-nawl*.

noo *or* **now, the** This is the common Scots form of *now*. In Glasgow speech an intrusive *s* can often be heard, creating such variants as **s'now, isnow,** or even **the snow**: 'Are we gaun isnow?' It's almost as if it was 'this now' which is being said, but it may be more to do with a contraction of 'just now'.

no real Literally, not real, this is used to mean outrageous, insane, unbelievable, and so on: 'Did ye hear that wee bampot diggin up the Big Man? The boay's pure no real.'

nosey To **do one's nosey** is to act inquisitively, look around a place pryingly: 'Have you got nothin better to do than come round here doin yer nosey?'

nougat (pronounced *nugget*) A wafer filled with mock cream and coated with chocolate, as served with ice-cream. A **single nougat** consists of one of these with a slab of ice-cream sandwiched between it and a plain wafer. For real gannets, a **double nougat** is the same thing but with the plain wafer replaced by another nougat.

no-user (the second part rhymes with *juicer*) A contemptuous term for a good-for-nothing or shiftless individual: 'Ah'd hate tae see ye turn oot a big no-user like yer aul man, son.'

nuchin Pronounced with the *ch* as in *loch*, this is a local variant of *nothing*, popular perhaps because the *ch* sound lends it added vehemence: 'And what dae Ah get out a this? Nuchin!'

nugget A slang word for a pound coin: 'Ah hate havin a pocket fulla nuggets. It pure ruins the line a yer strides.'

nuhin In broad Glasgow speech another variant of *nothing*: 'There nuhin left.'

numpty An idiot: 'See you? Ye're a grade-wan numpty; flyin colours, nae resits!'

nut A version of *no*, most often used on its own in reply to a question: 'Ah asked him if he wis comin oot for a dauner, an all he said wis "Nut."'

nyaff A disparaging term for a despicable or irritating person, especially one small in stature: 'Tell that wee nyaff Ah'm gauny boot his arse fae here tae Govan.' The word seems to derive from an older Scots term for the bark of a little dog. Interestingly enough though, Partridge's *Dictionary of Slang* refers to a Parisian slang word *gniaffe* (a term of abuse for a man) which would have a similar pronunciation. Perhaps the Académie Française would cite this as an example of the Auld Alliance corrupting the French language.

nyuck A disparaging term for anyone you dislike, for whatever reason: 'That wis a right shower a nyucks sittin in fronty us at the ballet last night.'

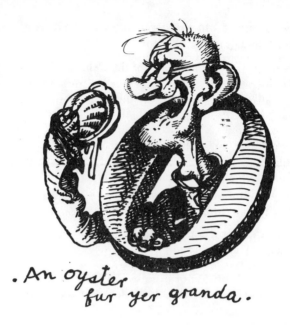

. An oyster fur yer granda.

oary boat A local term for a *rowing boat*: 'Sure Bonnie Prince Charlie went tae Skye in an oary boat? Ah seen it oan the telly.'

off The phrase **for the off** has several meanings:
1. about to leave, departing: 'Is that you for the off? Ah'll see ye doon the road.'
2. being dismissed from a job: 'Ah hear there's five ae us fur the off.'
3. about to die: 'Wan merr fright like yon an Ah'll be for the off.'

offie A familiar term for an off-licence: 'If the offies are shut we'll just need to get a few cans out the pub.'

offski A slang way of saying off, as in departing: 'Wan merr cup a coffee an Ah'm offski.'

old *or* **auld** Used in various combinations meaning *father*. **old boy, old man, old fella. Old yin** can be mother or father. **Old**

dear, old doll, old girl all mean *mother*. 'Tell yer old dear wee Mrs Brannigan was askin for her.'

Old Firm, the A nickname for the Celtic and Rangers football clubs when thought of together as traditional rivals: 'The Old Firm have been drawn together in the next round of the Cup.'

on To tell someone **you're not on** is to say there is no chance of your complying with his wishes: 'If ye think Ah'm gauny carry the can fur this baws-up ye're not on, sunbeam.'

onion bag A football journalists' cliché for the net of a goal: 'The boys in blue rattled three into the onion bag.'

ony *or* **olny** Two local versions of *only*: 'There's ony wan left an you're no gettin it.'

oot scoot A phrase of dismissal, usually said to children who are in the speaker's way: 'Here, let me in that cupboard, weans. Oot scoot, beat it!'
  This probably comes from a children's game in which players are eliminated in turn by means of a chant ending 'oot scoot, you're oot.'

ooyah A cry of pain, obviously just stopping short of calling 'you' something unprintable: 'Is that pie too hot yet? Ooyah!'

opposed A verbal distortion of *supposed* in the sense 'meant': 'Ye're not opposed tae park here, so ye're no.'

outsider Not a social outcast but any of the two thicker, often crustier, end slices of a loaf of bread: 'D'ye want this ootsider on yer piece?'

over it A local shortening of the common phrase 'over the moon', meaning delighted: 'Ah wis pure over it when Ah heard!'

ovies A familiar abbreviation of overalls: 'Aw maw, ye never washed ma ovies fur us!'

oyster A mouth-stretching delicacy obtainable from ice-cream sellers, consisting of two round shallow containers (like two halves of an oyster shell) made of the same stuff as wafers. One half is filled with ice-cream and the other placed on top to seal it. As this is far from being enough for the infamous Glasgow sweet tooth, one of the half-shells already contains a portion of artificial cream and is partly-coated with coconut-sprinkled chocolate: 'Run out to the icey an get us aw a pokey-hat – an ye better get an oyster fur yer granda.'

A bum like a peemet...

P45 This, of course, is the form given to a worker by an employer who is sacking him. In slang it is used when a person gets rid of a boyfriend or girlfriend: 'Ach, him? Ah gied him his P45 last week.'

pa *or* **paw** Both used locally to mean *father*. 'Tell yer pa his tea's oot.' 'Could ye go another wee goldie, Paw?'

Paddy's Market The well-known street market, just off The Briggait, which gained its name through being frequented by impecunious Irish immigrants. Its rough-and-ready appearance and the miscellaneousness of the goods on offer (everything from a secondhand wean's cardigan to a genuine Charles Rennie Mackintosh fireplace) ensured its use in comparisons with any untidy place: 'He's got the hoose lik Paddy's Market since she went inty the hospital.'

Paisley The phrase **get off at Paisley** means to practise *coitus interruptus*. 'He said it wid be awright, he wid get aff at Paisley, an now look at us!' This idea of 'not going all the way' is based

114

on a train journey back to Glasgow from the Clyde Coast, Paisley being the last stop before Glasgow Central.

A **Paisley screwdriver** is a jocular term for a hammer, implying, of course, that the inhabitants of this neighbouring borough are none too bright.

pally ally (rhyming with *Sally*) A nickname for pale ale, being a deliberate mispronunciation of the words: 'If the exports are Phil's, the lagers are Irene's, whose are the pally allies?'

pamp **To pamp** the horn of a car is to blow it: 'Ah hate these folk that have tae pamp their horn when they're goin away.' **A pamp** is an instance of doing this: 'He said tae wait ootside an gie the horn a pamp.'

pan **To pan** something is to break or burst it: 'Sumdy's panned the chippie's windy in.' It can also mean to damage something deliberately and systematically, as for example breaking all the windows and lights of a car: 'The moneylender sent two guys wi hammers roon tae pan his motor.'

To **pan someone's melt in** is to give him a severe beating.

Someone who works very hard at a task is often said to **knock** his **pan in**: 'They pay ye buttons an expect ye tae knock yer pan in.'

panel A person who is unfit for work through illness and has been certified as such by a GP (given a **panel line**) is often said to be **on the panel**: 'He's been on the panel all week an he's climbin the walls.' The original meaning of the phrase was that a person had been accepted onto a doctor's *panel* of patients who were treated free of charge.

panhandler A slang word for someone who is always scrounging, attempting to borrow money or goods: 'You're that saft, ye haun oot money tae any aul panhandler that asks ye.'

pan loaf This kind of bread, having a light crust all round it, gave its name to a posh way of speaking: a **pan-loaf accent**. Some say this is because pan loaves were more expensive than plain loaves; others explain it by suggesting that *pan loaf* is Glasgow rhyming slang for *toff* (pronounced *toaff*).

Pansy Potter A nickname bestowed on any female who performs a task requiring some physical strength: 'Look at Pansy Potter humphin they suitcases up the stair hersel.' This comes from 'Pansy Potter, the Strongman's daughter', apparently a cartoon character in a children's comic.

See also **Pansy Potters** in Rhyming slang.

pants Used in slang to mean:
    1. rubbish, no good: 'Have ye heard their latest wan? It's pure pants, man!'
    2. very easy, no bother: 'There's nothin tae it . . . it's a skoosh . . . it's pants!'

pap[1] This is used as a verb to mean *throw*. 'He papped a snowball at a polis motor.' Similarly, **pap out** means throw out: 'She went to Strathclyde Uni but they papped her out after a year.'

pap[2] A fool or soft character: 'Imagine a lassie a mines gaun aboot wi a pap lik yon.' The word originally meant a woman's breast or nipple and has thus been adapted in the same way as *diddy*.

papa Another name for a grandfather: 'See if yer papa wants another cup a tea.' Sometimes the grandsire's name is added, to avoid confusion where more than one is still to the fore: 'It's no Papa Ronnie that's takin ye; it's Papa John.'

pape Shortened from *papist*, this is a fairly offensive term for a Roman Catholic.

Paradise A nickname used by Celtic supporters for their home ground at Parkhead.

paralytic Often pronounced *paralettic*, this means extremely drunk: 'He disny think he's hud a good night if he disny end up paralytic.'

parish This turns up in two somewhat old-fashioned phrases. Someone who is **on the parish** is receiving unemployment or other benefits. Billy Connolly sang a song about various people going to **join the parish**, that is, register for such financial support. The expressions are relics from former times when each parish was responsible for looking after its own poor.

Parkhead Also known as Celtic Park, this is the home ground of Celtic F. C.: 'Ah hear they've ordered a bigger biscuit tin up at Parkhead.'

parkie A familiar term for a park-keeper: 'Ask that parkie what time they shut the gates.'

Parly Road A familiar name for Parliamentary Road, in the city centre: 'Her man got knocked doon wi a blue bus in Parly Road the other week.'

Partick The name of this district on the north-west side of the Clyde is found in the proverbial phrase **before the Lord left Partick**, meaning a very long time ago: 'Her faimly's steyed up this close since before the Lord left Partick. We're in this buildin twinty year an we're still the new folk tae her.'

Why Partick should be singled out as God-forsaken I cannot say, unless it has something to do with the area's high density of Glasgow University students.

party song Not a piece of musical jollification but an anthem of sectarian bigotry, as most often performed by devotees of football teams that attract such supporters: 'Right youse. Wan merr a yer party songs an yeez're aw barred.'

patter Your **patter** is what you have to say for yourself. If someone asks you to **gie's aw yer patter** this is a friendly invitation to expound some chat or pass on any news.

The term can also mean things said to impress others or amuse them: 'The guy's got mair patter than a double-glazin salesman.' 'Wait till ye hear her brother's patter . . . ye'll knot yersel!' **The patter** is used to mean the kind of language spoken by insiders: 'He knows aw the patter aboot computers an aw that.'

Two phrases used to express contempt for the standard of someone's patter are: **yer patter's like watter** and **yer patter's like toothpaste . . . it comes oot a tube.**

To patter away is to have a friendly conversation: 'Ah didny think they'd get on but the pair of them've been patterin away aw night.'

Someone who tries to impress others with his line in chat may be called a **patter-merchant**, and the term is also used for someone who thinks he is funny but isn't: 'Keep yer jokes to yourself if that's the best ye can do, patter-merchant.'

pawnies *or* **ponnies** A nickname for the card game pontoon: 'Let me put it this way, pal . . . if this was a game a pawnies you'd be burst.'

peever Another name for hopscotch or for the stone or flattened can that is kicked around in the game: 'Look at this: somebody's chalked out the beds for peever!'

pelmet Someone whose backside is regarded as sticking out somewhat may be said to sport **a bum like a pelmet.**

pelters Severe abuse or criticism: 'The councillor got pelters at the meeting about the new motorway.' 'They're aw giein us pelters aboot this carry-on an it's got hee-haw tae dae wi me.'

people The celebratory cry **We are the people!** is often heard from football fans, or another self-contained group, when they want to give vent to their feelings of superiority over the mass of humankind.

pep Short for peppermint cordial, ordered as a mixer in certain drinks: 'The old man likes his dark rum an pep on a cold night.'

petted lip A facial expression in which the lower lip sticks out, indicative of sulking: 'Look at the petted lip she's givin us . . . ye could hang out a washin on it!'

P. F., the A slang term and abbreviation for the Procurator Fiscal: 'Ah've got tae keep the heid doon till the P. F. gets aff ma back.'

photie A photograph: 'The first prize in the raffle's a signed photie of Daniel O'Donnell.'

D'ye want a photie? is a belligerent question asked by someone who feels that the person addressed has been staring at him.

piece A term that covers any sandwich or even a single slice of bread spread with something: 'The wean wants a piece an jam.' 'Ah'm fed up wi corn beef on ma pieces.' If a child asks for a piece and the person asked finds there is only bread but nothing to put on it, the child may be offered a **piece an breid**.

A **piecebox** or **piecetin** is a container in which a worker or a schoolchild carries his lunch: 'Aw naw! Ah'm away withoot ma piecebox!'

The phrase **put her on a piece an eat her** is a terribly unromantic suggestion often shouted at kissing couples, demonstrating local contempt and distrust for public displays of passion in which football and inebriation are not involved.

pig A cruel term used among males for an unattractive female: 'Hey Sammy, that wis a pure pig ye were winchin the other night.' An even more extreme form is a **pig wi knickers**.

If males are on the hunt for talent and they assess the bar or club they are in as being disappointing in that respect they may dismiss the place as a **pigs' ballroom**.

pint dish A slang term for a pint tumbler: 'Imagine drinkin Martini oot a pint dish. You've goat nae class, huv ye, ya toerag?'

pish A local version of *piss*. Also used to mean rubbish or nonsense: 'See you ... ye talk a lot a pish.' **Pished** means drunk: 'How did Ah end up talkin tae you? Jeez, Ah must be pished.'

To **rip the pish** out of someone is to make fun of him.

plab A nicely onomatopoeic word for a cow's dropping: 'Ever stepped on a big coo's plab wi sandals on? It gets aw in between yer toes.'

The term can be used for other varieties of excrement:

'You're oot enjoyin yersel an Ah'm stuck in here up tae the elbows in plabby nappies.'

place A person who loses his temper in an extreme manner is said to **lose the place**: 'Chill out, big man . . . nae need tae lose the place, eh?'

plank To **plank** something is to hide it somewhere: 'The doughheid planked his winnin lottery ticket somewhere an now he canny find it.' Such a hiding-place, or the stuff hidden in it, is called **a plank**: 'Yer Granny's got ginger snaps in a wee plank just for youse.'

To **plank something down** is to set it down heavily: 'He planked his big bahookie doon on the settee an said that wis him for the night.'

play Someone who **plays himself** is not starring in his own biopic but messing about, not getting anything useful done: 'It would help if yeez done some graftin instead a playin yersels.'

The phrase **Ah'm no playin** is often used by a petulant child withdrawing from a game because it has become too rough, the rules are not being respected, or some such reason: 'It's shots each, or Ah'm no playin.' When children fall out with friends they often say 'Ah'm no playin wi youse' as a rebuff. As with many childhood expressions, this is occasionally used jocularly by adults.

playpiece Any snack eaten by a child during school playtime, not necessarily (or even usually) a sandwich: 'Can Ah have a packet a crisps for ma playpiece?'

pleckie A slang shortening of *plectrum*, ie a guitar pick: 'He's crackin up cause he's lost the souvenir pleckie he got aff Kinky Friedman.'

plook *or* **pluke** A **plook** is a pimple or spot, especially on the face: 'If you don't shut it Ah'm gauny play dot-tae-dot wi yer plooks.' The term is also used as a contemptuous name: 'Ah don't know how she's gaun aboot wi a plook like him.'

To **plook** a pimple or spot is to squeeze it with the

fingers until it bursts: 'It hud a big yella heid oan it till Ah plookt it.'

   Plooky means pimply or covered in spots: 'He'd be no bad lookin if he wisny so plooky.'

plootered Yet another word meaning *drunk*: 'Leave the bam where he is. Serves him right for gettin plootered this early.'

plums The phrase **you're onto plums** is used to tell someone that he has been unsuccessful or there is nothing doing: 'If ye think ye're gettin a freebie aff me ye're onty plums, pal.' Why this pleasant fruit should be considered as second prize or undesirable I cannot tell. Some people substitute **a bag of plums** or even **rice** as what you are onto.

plunge To **plunge** someone is to stab him: 'Mind that rammy ootside the kebab bar last night? Ah hear a boay goat plunged.'

plunk A fairly old-fashioned word meaning to dodge school, play truant: 'Ah'd've got on better in life if Ah hadny plunked the school so much.' Someone who plays truant from school may be called a **plunker.**

pochle A **pochle** is any dishonest contest or business transaction: 'Aye an yer Christmas Draw's nuthin but a pochle every year!'

   To pochle something is to acquire it by means of a swindle or by cheating, or to be responsible for a fraud: 'She got her books for pochlin her expenses.'

podger A slang term meaning to have sexual intercourse with: 'Ah'd podger that aw right!'

pokey-hat A local term for an ice-cream cone: 'Get yer granda doon tae the café an he'll maybe buy ye a pokey-hat.'

polis This can mean the police ('Ah'm gauny get the polis tae youse'), an individual policeman or -woman ('He's no a bad big guy . . . fur a polis'), or a number of police officers ('Ah seen him runnin doon the back lane wi two polis on his tail').

A police station is often referred to as a **polis office** (pronounced *oaffis*): 'Ah'm phonin the polis office if youse don't turn doon that racket.'

The word also turns up in the phrase **murder polis** which can either be an exclamation of consternation or shock ('Murder polis! The weans've broke ma washin line!') or a description of a difficult or confused situation ('It'll be murder polis gaun tae work the morra if they don't get these roads gritted').

Polomint City A nickname, which was originally coined by CB enthusiasts but which spread to wider use, for East Kilbride. This comes from the exceptional proliferation of roundabouts encountered when driving through it: 'He wis last heard of in Polomint City tryin tae get onty the Motherwell Road.'

P. R., the A nickname and abbreviation for Paisley Road West, a main thoroughfare on the south-west bank of the Clyde: 'If ye get onty the P. R. any bus'll take ye inty toon.'

Priestie, the A nickname for the Priesthill area in the South Side: 'She got a cooncil flat in the Priestie efter her man goat aff his mark.'

problem The phrase **What's *your* problem?** is not intended to express a willingness to help but is actually a hostile challenge.

prod *or* **proddy** The word *Protestant* is commonly pronounced *prodestant* and these terms are shortenings of that: 'The proddies aw go tae that school.' 'Is that a Tim name or a Prod wan?'

Prosecutin Fiscal An alternative title for the Procurator Fiscal, commonly used amongst those who have cause to see his role in this light: 'Ah never done nuthin. Ah'm complainin tae the Prosecutin Fiscal aboot this.'

Provvy Cheque A slang term for a cheque issued by Provident Personal Credit Ltd.: 'Evrubdy roon here gets the Christmas prezzies wi a Provvy Cheque.'

This is a credit arrangement whereby someone borrows (at interest) a sum from this company, the funds being supplied as a cheque to be exchanged for goods at a shop that displays a sign indicating that it accepts such cheques.

puff candy A type of confection of a hard, crumbly consistency that tends, as I recall, to stick to the teeth (of which it is no doubt highly destructive). The term is used, especially by schoolkids, to mean easily done, no bother: 'That test was pure puff candy, Miss.' It is sometimes shortened to **puff**: 'C'mon, this'll be puff.'

puggled If a person is described as **puggled** this can mean he is mildly drunk or simply daft.

puggy This word turns up in various situations concerning money. It can be the kitty in a card game: 'The puggy's a fiver each, right?' **A puggy** can also be a one-armed bandit or other kind of gambling machine: 'It's no much fun goin for a pint wi a guy that just wants tae staun at that stupit puggy aw night.' The same term is used for a cash dispenser, almost as if every now and again you might get more money than you expect: 'Ah wis gauny pay ye back the noo but Ah couldny find a puggy that wis workin.'

To take a puggy is to become extremely angry: 'Keep the heid ... ye'll never get it sortit if ye take a puggy at it lik that.'

Someone who is highly inebriated or who has eaten too much may be described as **full as a puggy**. Similarly, if a person makes a habit of such overindulgence he may end up as **fat as a puggy**.

Puggy work means hard physical labour, the same as donkey work: 'It's awright fur you sittin on yer arse giein oot yer orders, an it's me that's tae dae the puggy work.'

pump Obviously onomatopoeic, this means fart: 'Who pumped?' 'Was that a wee pump I heard?'

pun A pound in weight: 'Run doon tae the fruit shoap an get us a pun a carrots an three pun a totties, there's a good wee soul.'

The phrase **there's no two pun a her hingin the right way** is a graphic way of saying that someone is oddly shaped.

punny *or* **punny eccy** School slang, used by both staff and pupils, for a punishment exercise, i.e. a written piece of work given to a child as punishment for some classroom crime: 'Ah canny come oot till Ah've finished this punny eccy for Aul Kipper.'

punt-up *or* **puntie-up** To give someone this is to help him get over a wall or on top of some obstacle by standing with your back to it and making a kind of stirrup with your interlaced fingers for the climber to put a foot into: 'You gie me a puntie-up an Ah'll pull ye up efter me.'

pure Used as an adjective or adverb, this has got nothing to do with being pristine but means total, totally, absolute, absolutely: 'She went pure mental when she heard.' 'That's a pure brilliant idea!' 'You are pure sad, pal.'

Comin doon the Queenie? The model boats are on the pond the day...

Queenie, the A familiar name for the Queens Park, a large public park on the South Side: 'Comin doon the Queenie? The model boats are on the pond the day.'

queer In the phrase **a queer difference** the word means great, not strange: 'There's a queer difference between the top line and what you come away with in your hand.'

queerie Any odd or eccentric individual: 'Ah've always thought her man was a bit of a queerie.'

queued out A term used to describe any place or event that is very busy or crowded: 'We tried tae get inty the Odeon tae see that *Braveheart II*, but when we seen it wis queued oot we jist came away.'

quoted This term comes from the world of betting and refers to the odds quoted by the bookies for certain racehorses or other competitors. In everyday speech **well-quoted** means highly-thought-of or respected: 'Ah hear that councillor you've got's well-quoted.'

The opposite of this is **not quoted**, i.e. not reckoned as being up to much: 'As for you, you're no quoted in this business so shut yer yap.'

Rab Haw, the Glesga Glutton...

ra In broad Glaswegian the word *the* often comes out as **ra**: 'Whit d'ye make a ra boays the day?'

Rab Ha' *or* **Haw** A name applied to any glutton or even to someone who merely has a big appetite: 'Ah went tae get merr soup but Rab Ha' here had snaffled the lot.'

Rab Ha', or Robert Hall, was a real person, a vagrant who died in 1843 having become famous throughout the west of Scotland for his unparallelled eating capacity. His rapacious appetite was often the subject of wagers and it seems that the smart money was always on Rab. The story is told of one such occasion when Rab was tasked with consuming a whole calf (except for the skin). The unfortunate beast was served up to Rab in the form of pies, which he duly despatched. Rab was then heard to ask where was this calf he was meant to be eating.

As well as being used as the name for more than one Glasgow restaurant, Rab is commemorated in the following rhyme:

Rab Ha' the Glesga Glutton
et ten loaves an a leg a mutton.

rag Someone who loses his temper is sometimes said to **lose the rag**: 'The boay said it wis an accident . . . there nae need tae lose the rag.'

raging Extremely angry: 'Ah knew she'd be ragin, so Ah didny bother phonin.'

rammy A **rammy** is a violent disturbance or any busy or bustling crowd: 'That wis some rammy when they said the tickets were sold out.'
    To rammy is to take part in such a violent disturbance: 'There's too much rammyin at the football these days . . . an that's just the players'.'

randan Someone who is **on the randan** is on a spree of wild behaviour, usually involving debauchery and drunkenness: 'Is that your second sherry ye're on? It's well seen ye're on the randan the night.'

rare Used to describe anything excellent: 'Ye make a rare cuppa tea, hen.' 'Ye want tae have seen that fillum . . . it wis rerr!'

rat In a similar way to **ra** (*the*), **rat** is a broad Glaswegian form of *that*: 'See rat? Rat's terrible, so it is.'

rats Someone, usually a child, who is very lively or can't sit still may be compared to a **bag of rats**: 'Can you no sit at peace till Ah get yer anorak on? Ye're like a bag a rats the day.'

rattle **To rattle** a part of a person's body is to hit him there: 'Ah'll rattle yer lug if Ah catch ye!'
    To rattle around is to be up and about, present and lively: 'Ah thought she'd huv the weans doon by noo but they're still rattlin around.'

rebel song A song that celebrates the deeds of Irish Republicans: 'Ah don't think they make karaoke tapes wi rebel songs on them.'

red *or* **rid** Red raw is a term used to describe parts of one's person that, through being very cold or wet, are sore and reddened: 'The weans' hauns were rid raw when they came in from makin their snowman.'

Red rotten means very bad, absolute rubbish: 'That play he took us tae wis red rotten . . . there wis nae story tae it.'

red biddy See under **biddy**.

refreshment A **wee refreshment** is a euphemism for an alcoholic drink: 'We'll maybe partake of a wee refreshment on the way through to Edinburgh.' This has given rise to various jokey ways of describing drunkenness, such as **well-refreshed** or **over-refreshed**: 'The club has received complaints that over-refreshed patrons are making too much noise when leaving the premises.'

Riddrie Hilton, the A nickname for H.M. Prison Barlinnie, located in the Riddrie area on the north-east side of Glasgow.

riddy A **riddy** is a red (or **rid**) face indicative of high embarrassment. It can also mean anything embarrassing: 'That wis a pure riddy when Ah drapped that plate.' To **take a riddy** is to blush: 'She took a big riddy when he walked in.'

riggin Rigging; a football slang term for the goal-net: 'McStay took wan look up an bang! it's in the riggin.'

right If a person wants to cast doubt on the likelihood or truth of something someone else has said he might say **that'll** (*or* **that will) be right**: 'What, work longer hours for the same money? Aye, that'll be right!' This expression is unusual in that it has a parallel in rhyming slang: **that'll be shining bright**. This is occasionally shortened to **that'll be shining**.

Right is also used to mean ready, all set: 'Are ye right? Come on then.'

rings Someone who is being violently sick is often said to be **vomiting rings round** himself. I suppose the idea is that the unfortunate individual is able to direct the flow away from his own person but is otherwise helpless: 'Ah don't know what he's been eatin, but he's been vomitin rings roon hissel aw mornin, the soul.'

rip Used in particular to mean to cut or slash someone with a blade: 'Ah'll rip ye wide, ya wee crapbag.'

ripped A slang word meaning under the influence of illicit drugs: 'Ye canny expect sense fae a guy that's ripped oot his nut hauf the time.'

road To be or get **in your own road** is to be very clumsy in performing some activity: 'Ah don't know what's up wi me the day. Ah'm just gettin in ma own road.'

On the road out, when applied to a person, means dying: 'Ah doubt that's her granmaw on the road out this time.'

roll about To laugh uproariously: 'Get um tae tell ye aboot when he got lost in Embra. We were aw rollin aboot when he telt us.'

rollie A hand-rolled cigarette: 'Look at the size a the rollie he's giein us! Ye'd need a poultice tae get a draw oot it.'

rooked Completely out of money, skint: 'We reckoned we'd taken enough money for the whole weekend but on Saturday mornin that was us rooked.'

room and kitchen A tenement flat, small, but a cut above a *single end* in that it has two rooms as well as a bathroom. One of the rooms has a cooker and sink and some occupants will use this room as a sitting room and keep the other room as a bedroom only. Other people are happy to sleep in the kitchen's bed-recess and use the other room as a sitting room.

Rossy A Glasgow pronunciation of Rothesay, Isle of Bute, traditionally popular as a holiday resort for citizens: 'Ma mammy says we're gaun tae Rossy oan the Waverley!'

rotten drunk Extremely drunk: 'Ah came in the door an nearly fell over the big waster lyin there rotten drunk.' This is sometimes shortened to **rotten**: 'No way is she gaun anywhere. She's pure rotten.'

Rottenrow, the The popular name for the Glasgow Royal Maternity Hospital, which is in a street called Rottenrow: 'Were you born in the Rottenrow as well?'

Roukie, the A familiar name for Rouken Glen, an extensive public park on the South Side: 'Does the thirty-eight bus still take ye the length o the Roukie, son?'

Royal, the A common abbreviation for the Royal Infirmary: 'She was a Sister in the Royal before she came to Yorkhill.'

rubber ear To **throw** or **sling someone a rubber ear** means to deliberately fail to hear someone, to ignore him pointedly, or to turn down someone who asks you out: 'Ah tried oot the patter on this wee doll but she slung us a rubber ear.'

Also used as a verb: '"No hard feelins" he says, the snidey get. Ah jist rubber-eared um.'

rubber man To **do a** or **one's rubber man** is to be so drunk that you cannot stand upright without swaying around, holding onto something, or looking as if your legs might buckle: 'Ah seen your wee brother daein his rubber man in George Square last night.'

Ruglonian A native of Rutherglen, which is often pronounced Ruglen: 'Don't cry me a Glaswegian, sonny boy. Ah'm a Ruglonian born an bred.'

rummle A **rummle in the sheets** is a less than romantic way to describe a sexual encounter: 'Know what the cheeky peasant says tae me? "Fancy a rummle in the sheets, doll?" Ah took ma haun aff his jaw.'

rumped An extremely short haircut is often said to have been **rumped right inty the wid**. See **wid²**.

run To **run about daft** is to be very busy, under pressure, especially if this involves going to and from several places: 'That wean's got me runnin aboot daft tryin tae get the right batteries for that game a his.'

Another version of this is **run about stupit**.

runnie Used especially by schoolchildren, to **take a runnie at** something is to take a run at it: 'Ah bet Ah could jump that waw if Ah took a runnie at it.'

run-out Someone who **does a run-out** is guilty of consuming a meal in a restaurant and leaving swiftly without settling the bill: 'D'ye hear aboot the Irish run-oot? They ordered a meal an ran oot withoot eatin it!'

. blaw the simmit aff ye .

sad Apart from its usual meanings this word is used, especially by schoolkids, to label anything unfair or unpleasant: 'When I tell you to do something, child, I'm afraid that "That's pure sad, Miss" is not an appropriate response.'

A **sad case** *or* **saddie** is a slang term for someone considered crazy, especially in a dangerous way: 'Did ye hear whit that big sad case done?'

Saltmarket The phrase **all the comforts of the Saltmarket** is a piece of irony meaning no comforts at all, no mod cons: 'Aw we're needin is a bit a carpet doon, the watter on, an somethin tae sit on an we'll have aw the comforts a the Saltmarket!'

This is a survival from the bad old days when this street running south from Glasgow Cross was infamous for its poverty.

sangwidge An odd version of *sandwich*: 'The French fancies do look nice but I think I'll just have a wee cheese sangwidge.'

sanny This can mean a sandshoe: 'Don't forget yer sannies for gym tomorrow.' It can also be a sandwich: 'Ah've et nuthin aw day but a packet a British Rail sannies.'

Sarry Heid The nickname of the Saracen's Head public house, in the Gallowgate, reputedly the oldest pub in the city, although the original building no longer stands. This pub is proverbial for hard drinking and boisterousness: 'We'll nick inty the Sarry Heid fur a coupla pints a shammy before we go inty the concert.'

Scabby Aggie An abusive name, particularly among school-children, for any female considered unclean: 'Don't tell us ye've tae sit next tae *that* Scabby Aggie?'

scabby touch Used in a children's game like tig. The difference is that it can begin spontaneously, as when someone is adjudged to have come into contact with something disgusting. He is then told he has the scabby touch and is obliged to touch someone else in order to pass on and free himself from the vile contagion: 'When Ah telt um Ah wis efter a refund he looked at us like Ah'd gied um the scabby touch.'

scadge A slang term for a tramp or a disreputable-looking person: 'Don't staun next tae us, ya scadge. Ye'll gie us a showin up.'
    The word sounds as if it might be connected with *scavenger*.

scheme A housing estate, especially any of the postwar council estates in such areas as Drumchapel or Darnley. Although great strides have been taken in improving these places they are still tarred with the brush of isolation and lack of amenities: 'There's no a street in the scheme that doesny have boarded-up windies.'

schemie (pronounced *skeemy*) A rather disparaging term for a person, especially a youth, who lives in a scheme: 'That pub's full of schemies on a Friday night.'

scooby If you **don't have a scooby** you don't have a clue, have no idea at all about the subject in question: 'Ah asked him if he knew how tae work it but he doesny have a scooby.' This comes from the rhyming slang for clue, **scooby doo**, inspired by the eponymous canine hero of an American children's cartoon series seen on TV in this country from the early 1970s onwards.

scoof A slang word meaning to steal, or take charge of something that seems to lack an obvious owner: 'When Ah came back fae the lavvy some ratbag hud scoofed the Safeways bag Ah left under ma seat.'

To **scoof** an empty house is to break into it and strip out everything of possible value, such as radiators, pipes, cables, etc: 'These flats wi the boarded-up windies have aw been scoofed long since.'

scone A name for a man's flat bunnet: 'Hang on till Ah stick ma scone on.'

Someone looking aggrieved or unhappy may be posed the unsympathetic question 'Who stole yer scone?'

scrappie A scrap-metal dealer, or his yard: 'Ah've seen motors in better nick than that lyin in a scrappie.'

scratcher A bed, obviously with the suggestion that it is inhabited by fleas as well as the nominal occupant: 'Ye'll be waitin long enough if ye're waitin fur that durty aul rascal tae get oot his scratcher.'

screw If you want someone to calm down or start behaving sensibly you might tell him to **screw the bobbin** or **screw the nut**: 'The gaffer's just lookin for an excuse tae get a few bodies oot the door, so ye better screw the nut here.'

screwtap A screwtop bottle, usually for beer: 'Dae ye still get big Whitbreads in screwtaps?' The most famous use of the term has to be in *Screwtaps are Fallin on ma Heid,* Matt McGinn's version of the Bacharach-David song *Raindrops Keep Falling on my Head.*

scud[1] Someone who is **in the scud** *or* **scuddy** is in the nude:

'The durty beasts were takin photies of each other in the scud!' **In the bare scud** means the same but suggests that the speaker is even more shocked. **Scuddy** is also sometimes used as an adjective: 'We went tae this beach an there was aw these scuddy punters stoatin aboot.'

A **scuddy book** is a pornographic magazine: 'Ah wis cleanin under his bed an fun a pile a scuddy books, the durty wee devil!'

scud² A slang term for wine: 'See's a bottle a Beck's an a glass a red scud.'

see Used to introduce the subject of remarks that immediately follow: 'See that wummin doon the stair? Talk aboot ignorant!' This is a useful device for people who like to break in a subject gradually rather than breenge straight to the point: 'See that guy wi the baseball hat, see his dug, see where it does its business? Shouldny be allowed.'

See if is used to introduce a question seeking information: 'See if Ah ask your pal for a len a his lawnmower, will he gie us it?' This can also be another way of saying *if*: 'See if Ah've tae tell you again, Ah'll tan yer erse.'

session A period spent drinking alcohol is often called a **session** *or* **bevvy session**: 'Ah used to go for lunch wi them till it startit turnin inty a session every time.' Some people shorten this to **sesh**: 'Know what Ah fancy? A right good-goin wee sesh wi ma mates.'

shady Used in slang to describe anything undesirable: 'Have we tae dae aw this fur the morra? That's pure shady, Miss!'

shape A disparaging term for anyone considered physically odd-looking: 'Did ye see that wee shape she ended up dancin wi?'

Shaws, the A familiar name for the Pollokshaws area, on the South Side: 'Oh him? He's wan a the queer folk a the Shaws.'

sheet To **put a sheet round** in a place of work is to make a collection of money for someone who may be leaving, getting married, having a baby, and so forth: 'Did ye hear? Aul Miseryguts isny lettin us put a sheet roon for wee Sheila.'

The cash so collected is known as **sheet money**: 'That sheet money came in awful handy for baby clothes.'

To **put to** (somebody's) **sheet** is to make your contribution: 'Right, emdy that hasny pit tae this sheet, get yer money in noo.'

The expression probably originated in the collection of cash or goods in an actual bedsheet carried round in a neighbourhood.

sherbet dab An inexpensive sweet for children: a paper bag containing some sherbet and a lollipop which the child licks and then dips into the sherbet.

sheuch *or* **shuch** (pronounced like *shuck,* but with the *ch* as in *loch*) A Scots word for ditch, used locally to mean the cleft of the buttocks: 'He gave um a toe-ender, right in the sheuch!'

The phrase **up the sheuch** means in a state of error, barking up the wrong tree: 'If that's what ye think, ye're up the sheuch, mate.'

Shields, the A familiar name for the Pollokshields area on the South Side: 'Is the Shields no a dry area?' 'If it is Ah know the guy that drank it dry.'

shilling This pre-decimal coin lives on in the phrases **not the full shilling** and **threepence off the shilling**, which both mean 'not right in the head', not possessed of a fully functioning brain.

shirrackin Someone who gets a **shirrackin** is being given a row, a severe reprimand: 'Her Maw gied her a good shirrackin for no comin in last night.'

shite-awful Of extremely low quality: 'Efter aw that big build-up it wis a shite-awful gemme.'

shiters To **put the shiters up** a person is to terrify him: 'Tell him ye're gauny shop him, just tae put the shiters up the wee nyaff.'

shoodery One step up from a coal-carry, that is, the person carried is positioned on the carrier's **shooders** (shoulders), with a leg on each side of the carrier's neck: 'Her boyfriend was giein her a shoodery so's she could see the stage an the big eejit went an drapt her.'

Shooey *or* **Shoo; Shuggy** *or* **Shug** For some unexplained reason Glaswegians often insert a phantom *s* in pronouncing certain words beginning with *h*. The name Hugh is one of these: 'Her man was Sir Shoo Fraser's chauffeur.' That takes care of **Shooey** and **Shoo**, but what about **Shuggy** and **Shug**, which are both also nicknames for Hugh?

shoot To **shoot** means to leave, especially quickly: 'Ah'll need tae shoot in a couple of minutes.' This is shortened from the phrase **shoot the crow** which means the same thing: 'He shot the crow before we got back.' I don't know why firing at a bird should be equated with departure; some say it is rhyming slang, ie *shoot the crow* for *go*, but this doesn't work when, as often happens, people say 'shoot the *craw*'.

shot Used in slang to mean any item or individual. For example, a Highlandman might be referred to as 'an Angus Og shot', and a homosexual as a 'bent shot': 'Do you want the twenty-five or fifty pence size?' 'Gie's the ten-bob shot.'

This probably comes from betting parlance, in which, say, a horse starting at odds of 10–1 would be a 'ten-to-one shot'.

shots each A local expression meaning turn and turn about: 'There's only wan joystick between yeez, so it's tae be shots each, right?'

shout To **shout** someone is to call him, alert him to something, such as the fact that it's time for him to get up: 'Ma Maw shouts us at hauf six.' 'Shout us when we get to Thornwood Drive, will you please, driver?'

To **shout on** a person is to call out his name: 'There sumdy shoutin on you round the back.'

shows, the A funfair or carnival: 'We all went to the shows at Bellahouston Park.'

shuffle An old-fashioned slang term for a betting shop: 'See if ye're passin the shuffle, gauny stick this line oan fur us?'

shuge A Glaswegian variant of *huge*, undergoing the same change in pronunciation as *Hugh*: 'Sumdy's dug a big shuge hole in the road.'

shunk *or* **shunkie** Slang words for a toilet: 'Ma eyeballs are floatin. Mind ma pint till Ah dive tae the shunk.'
    It may be that there is a connection between this usage and the well-known manufacturer of sanitary ware, Shanks.

shy A **shy** is a throw-in in a game of football: 'The big donkey's last shot was that far off the mark it went out for a shy on the other side.' **To shy** the ball is to use it in a throw-in: 'He shied it right inty the goalmouth.'

sick Someone who takes time off work because of illness is said to be **on the sick**.
    To **sicken someone's happiness** is to spoil their fun, make their life a misery: 'Would it no sicken yer happiness havin tae go hame tae a greetin face like that?'
    A **sickener** is something bad that happens to a person, something that is a huge disappointment: 'The very next week after she changed her lottery numbers they came up. What a sickener!'
    If someone believes that they have won an argument they might crow over their opponent by saying to them: **sickened you!**

sideyways This can mean sideways: 'It'll no go that way; we'll need to try it sideyways.' It is also a jocular version of suicide: 'If that car alarm doesny stoap soon Ah'm gauny commit sideyways!'

signwriter A slang term for an unemployed person is a **signwriter for the Social Security**, i.e. someone who signs on.

sillywatter Like **cheekywatter**, a name for alcoholic drink that includes an indication of how it is conceived as affecting the consumer: 'Whit? Have you been on the sillywatter? Gie's a break!'

simmit This Scots word for vest appears in various proverbial phrases. For example, of a very powerful alcoholic drink it may be said that **it wid blaw the simmit aff ye**.

An ironic remark made by a person who remains untouched by a purportedly moving story is **it wid fair tear yer simmit.**

sin Anything that is regarded as unjust or pitiable may be described as **a sin**: 'The wee soul had tae walk hame in that snaw; a sin, so it wis.'

sine-died A slang term meaning permanently barred: 'He's sayin there's nae way you're gettin back in there. Ye're sine-died, he says.' This comes from the football practice (never very common, it seems) of banning for life a player who has committed some unforgiveable offence (*sine die* being Latin, literally, for 'without a day').

singin Like *laughing* this is often used to mean very happy or lucky: 'If this weather keeps up till the weekend we're singin.'

singin ginger See **ginger**.

single (often pronounced *sing*-ull) On a chip-shop menu, anything with the word **single** in front of it is sold on its own, without chips: 'Gies a single fish, two pokes a chips, an a deep-fried Mars Bar.'

A **single** is a loose cigarette, sold individually in some shops to those not in funds: 'Here Ah'm gaspin fur a drag an Ah huvny the price ae a tipped single.'

single end A local term for a one-room tenement flat: 'Ah wis dragged up in a single-end in Maryhill an look at us noo.'

sink To **sink the boot on** someone is to kick him: 'The dirty big animal sunk the boot on the goalie when he was on the deck.'

In football, to **sink** a player is to bring him down with a hard tackle: 'Sumdy sink that wee striker for goodness sake!'

sinker A descriptive term for a dirty look or the kind of glance that makes the receiver feel like crawling away to hide: 'The guy wouldny shut up till wee Elspeth drew him a right sinker.'

sittie-doon *or* **sittie-in** Applied to a meal, these mean the opposite of carry-out: 'It's no often Ah get taken oot for a sittie-doon dinner.'

skate If you win something easily you might be said to **skate** it: 'The Jags'll skate that gemme the morra.'

skelf A **skelf** can be a sliver of wood that gets stuck under the skin, especially, but not exclusively, of a finger or toe: 'Ah told ye ye would get skelfs in yer bum if ye sat on that fence.' It can also mean a very skinny or undersized person: 'Imagine Big Gus bein married tae a wee skelf like her.'

skelly A term applied to a person whose eyes cross or who has a squint: 'Look at yer Granny gaun skelly tryin tae thread that needle.'

skelp This Scots word for smack is also used locally in the phrase **skelp it**, meaning to work briskly at a job: 'We'll need tae skelp it tae get this finished by dinnertime.'

  On the skelp means on a wild night out or drinking spree: 'Some state he's in. He looks like he's been on the skelp for a week.'

skinto A local variant of skint, i.e. out of money: 'OK, wan merr can a ginger each an that's yer lot, or ye'll have yer aul granda skinto.'

skip Someone who **skips** something, especially paying for something, gets away with avoiding it: 'They school weans aw pile on the bus at the wan time an the hauf a them skip their fares.'

skitter A **skitter** can mean a small amount of something: 'There only a wee skitter a milk left in the jug.'

skittery Used to describe anything considered small or contemptible: 'Ah'm still starvin after that skittery wee helpin ye gave us.'

It is also applied to food or drink that it is feared may cause diarrhoea: 'They curries are too skittery for me.'

skitterywinter Traditionally, a name applied to the last person to turn up for work in a factory, shipyard, office etc., on Hogmanay (in some workplaces, also on Fair Friday). The unfortunate latecomer would be greeted by his workmates banging loudly on any suitable surface. The term is still heard in wider use to mean anyone who is dilatory or lags behind: 'How is it you're always the last out yer pit, skitterywinter?'

skoosh Any fizzy soft drink: 'Ah could murder a big boatle a skoosh!'

A **skoosh** or **skoosh-case** is something that is done with no great effort: 'Ah tried tae convince aul greetin-face the flittin would be a skoosh-case but ye can tell her nuthin.'

To skoosh something or **skoosh it** is to accomplish it with ease: 'Just concentrate on yer three-point turns an ye'll skoosh that drivin test.'

Skooshed is another word for drunk: 'He wis that skooshed ye couldny make oot a word he wis sayin.'

slabberchops A name to call someone, especially a baby, who salivates or dribbles: 'Put a bib on wee Slabberchops or that Babygro'll be soakin in five minutes.'

slag To insult or make uncomplimentary remarks about a person is **to slag** him: 'Never mind them slaggin ye ... they're pig-ignorant, the lot a them.' A **slag** is an insulting remark.

A **slag-name** is a derogatory nickname given by schoolkids to one another.

slaughtered A slang word for drunk: 'Ah knew Ah wis totally slaughtered when Ah startit singin songs an forgettin everythin after the first line.'

sluch To eat or drink something, especially soup, making noises with one's mouth: 'He gies ye a right showin up wi his sluchin.'

slug **To slug** a liquid is to drink it straight from the bottle: 'Could you no use a glass instead of sluggin it oot the boatle?'
   A slug is a drink from a bottle: 'Gie's a slug a that skoosh before ye finish it.'

slush A nickname for tea: 'Wait an Ah'll stick the kettle on for a wee cup a slush.'

smell To make something, usually the breath, smell of something: 'Eatin that garlicky food really smells yer breath.'

snakie Short for snakebite, the drink concocted of cider and lager: 'If she's been on the snakies aw night it's nae wunner she's honkin her load.'

snotter Someone who has a cold or a runny nose may have it said of him that **the snotters are blindin** *or* **trippin him.**

snottery Used as a general term of disapproval or contempt: 'Is that snottery wee drap aw the tea that's left?' 'What's that snottery aul get lookin at us fur?'

snotterybeak A name to call someone with a runny nose: 'That sniffin's drivin me up the waw. Wid sumdy gie Snotterybeak a len ae a hanky?'

snyster A term used to mean any little bite of something tasty, especially something sweet: 'Ah could just go a wee snyster afore ma tea.'

so A common local usage is the instant confirmation of something you have just said (a double positive?) by means of phrases beginning with *so*: 'Ah'm gettin right fed up wi this, so Ah am.' 'That hat suits ye, so it does.'
   So I will is an ironic phrase seeming to express agreement but actually meaning the opposite: 'You've to have this finished for tomorrow.' 'Aye, an so Ah wull.'

soapdogger An insult, implying a lack of personal hygiene brought about by avoiding soap. See **dog.**

Society man, the Not someone who moves in refined circles, but a local term for a representative of the Co-operative Insurance Society who calls to collect periodical policy payments: 'Is this no the night for the Society man?'

sodie Soda. 'Ah could just go a wee sodie scone.' 'Ye get a rare loaf a sodie breid oot that bakers.' 'See's a Remy an sodie watter, barman.'

Sons of William A collective term for Protestants (especially Rangers supporters), deriving, of course, from their hero William of Orange: 'Bemused citizens looked on as an advance party of the Sons of William took over one of the city-centre bars in anticipation of tomorrow night's European Cup game.'

sook To call a person **a sook** is to accuse him of being a toady, trying to ingratiate himself with his superiors: 'Ah bet you've finished yer homework already, ya wee sook.'

   To sook in is to try to ingratiate yourself with someone in authority over you: 'There would be merr work done aroon here if you put in a full shift instead a spendin hauf yer time sookin in wi the gaffer.'

   Sookie sweeties are hard sweets, like boilings, that have to be sucked rather than chewed: 'Mind an get yer Granny sookie sweeties . . . she canny go the caramels wi they new wallies.'

Sooside, the The area of Glasgow south of the river Clyde: 'Ma Maw'll no move away fae the Sooside.' An inhabitant of this area is called a **Soosider.**

sore hand A large jam sandwich. The joke is in comparing the combination of white bread and red jam with a bloodstained bandage:

sore wan A painful injury: 'The wean got a right sore wan runnin inty that glass door.'

soul (sometimes rhymes with *howl*) This is a term expressing affection or pity for another person: 'She's that happy wi her new dolly, the wee soul.' 'Could somebody no gie that poor aul soul a haun across the road?'

144

Spam Valley A disparaging term for any suburban area of good housing and amenities in which live many people, especially younger couples, who have trouble affording it. Such people are said to have to economise to the extent of being obliged to include lots of Spam in their diet: 'A cheap and cheerful café-bar popular with the local Spam Valley set.'

spare A general term for unattached members of the opposite sex: 'There's always plenty of spare at Big Mandy's parties.'

special A name used by various brewers for their heavy beers: 'They've only got special or lager on draught.' **Spesh** is a shortened form of this: 'Two pints a spesh when ye're ready, Tony.'

specky A term applied to any spectacle-wearing person: 'Hey, Specky! Pass us that ashtray.' 'Ah thought her man would be nice-lookin, no a specky wee nyaff.'

Spiders, the A nickname for Queen's Park F. C., deriving from the fact that the black-and-white-hoops on their jerseys are reminiscent of a spider's web. Although not in the top flight of Glasgow clubs, Queen's Park have a long history and their home ground, Hampden Park, is the national stadium.

spinbin A slang word for a psychiatric hospital: 'Ye still workin in the spinbin?'

spittin feathers A slang term meaning dry-mouthed, extremely thirsty: 'Brilliant, eh? Ye come in from half a shift in the garden, spittin feathers, an some lazy bassa's swallied aw the lagers.'

spur The phrase **take the spur** means to become annoyed, take offence: 'C'mon, Ah'm only kiddin ye. Nae need tae take the spur.'

squaddie A schoolteachers' term for a P. E. teacher. Perhaps this originated in the fact that many of these are (or were traditionally) ex-servicemen.

square go See under **go.**

square sausage A local name for Lorne sausage, sausage meat formed into a rough oblong and then cut into slices: 'Ma aunty in Canada says there's a shop in Toronto that sells square sausage an Irn Bru.' Strangers to Glasgow are often surprised to find they are eating this instead of a link when they order a roll and sausage.

squid A gallus version of quid, that is, a pound sterling: 'Ah'm doon tae two squid an a haunfu a mince.'

squinty A local version of *squint,* meaning crooked or askew: 'Only a bum joiner would leave the thing lookin as squinty as that.'

stairhead (often pronounced *sterrheid*) This is the name given in tenement closes to the landing at the top of each flight of stairs. A **stairhead toilet** was a communal lavatory on such a landing in the days before inside facilities became the norm. As you might expect, a **stairhead window** is a window at a stairhead: 'It's freezin in that close wi the sterrheid windy open.'

stakes Another term borrowed from the world of gambling, in this case from the titles of horse races, such as the *Queen Elizabeth II Stakes.* In local slang this is used to give a descriptive name to any situation: 'If Ah canny get ma hauns oan some readies afore the end a the month it'll be pure desperation stakes.'

stank A street drain, or the metal grille that covers it: 'Ah drapt a pound coin an it rolled doon that stank.' The phrase **doon the stank** is used in the same way as the English *down the drain*: 'It's just money doon the stank tryin tae keep that place gaun.'
   Stankie is a children's game of marbles that makes use of the grille of a round stank as a playing surface, handy because the marbles sit neatly in the holes: 'We canny get playin stankie cause the gutter's choked.'

stank-dodger A slang term for a skinny person, implying that such individuals have to avoid street drains for fear of falling down one: 'What's a stank-dodger like you need tae be on a diet fur?'

steakie A steak knife: 'The mad bastart went fur us wi a steakie.'

steam There are several Glasgow expressions connected with this word, perhaps reflecting the city's historical links with the construction of ships and railway engines.

To get steamed in to a thing or a person is to set about it or him with great vigour: 'If we get steamed in to this paper-strippin we'll manage a pint before they shut.' 'The boy took a pure maddy an got steamed inty the pair a them.'

Someone who has **a good head of steam about him** is obviously elevated by drink, like a steam engine stoked up and ready to chug along: 'You had a good head a steam about ye when Ah bumped inty ye that night.'

A steamer is a slang term for a drinking bout: 'When wis the last time you *wereny* on a steamer on a Friday night?'

Someone who is drunk may be described as **steamin** or **steamin drunk**: 'If comin in steamin drunk every night is his plan he'll be oot that door.' **Steamed** or **steamed up** are similarly used: 'They get steamed up on the cheap wine an go lookin for bother.'

steamboats Another word for drunk: 'Ah've seen the guy totally steamboats in the middle of the day.' Some say that the origin of this picturesque expression lies in the traditional Glasgow pastime of going for pleasure-cruises down the Firth of Clyde. Apparently, men would give the excuse of 'going to take a look at the engines' to pay a visit to the bar. It then became proverbial that people alighting from such steamboat trips would seem to have difficulty in regaining their land legs.

steamie A local name for a public laundry, formerly common all over the city but now mostly a thing of the past. As Tony Roper's popular play *The Steamie* showed to perfection these places were often the hub of their community and renowned as hotbeds of gossip, and it is this aspect of their existence that lives on in the phrase **the talk of the steamie**, applied to anything or anyone considered scandalous: 'She's the talk of the steamie the way she carries on.'

steelies A slang term for steel-toecapped protective working boots: 'Ah'd like tae get inty that toerag's heid wi ma steelies.'

stenked Yet another word for drunk. A philologist might have a field day investigating why so many of these begin with *st-*.

stiffen To batter a person, especially to knock him unconscious: 'Ah'll stiffen the both of yeez if ye don't cut oot the argy-bargyin.' I suppose the idea is really that the attacked person will be killed and thus undergo rigor mortis.

stinkin rotten Literally, rotted to the point of becoming smelly, this is used to describe anything considered very bad: 'She telt us that wis a good story, an here it wis wan a the most stinkin rotten books Ah ever opened.'

stir Someone who deliberately causes trouble between others is said to **stir it**: 'Never mind what that wee cow says. She's just tryin tae stir it.' A **stirrer** is a person who behaves in this manner. When someone wants to tell another person that a third party in their company is stirring it this can be done silently by miming the motions of stirring a pot.

stoat The local pronunciation of the Scots *stot*, meaning bounce: 'Gauny no stoat yer baw ootside this windy? Yer da's goat a sair heid.'

In betting circles the word is used to mean win, as in: 'If this line stoats Ah'll get ye a doner kebab.'

Stoat doon is what particularly heavy rain is said to do: 'It wisny takin the time tae rain . . . it wis stoatin doon.'

To stoat aboot is to circulate, move around in a not particularly purposeful manner: 'Her an her mammy like tae stoat aboot the shops on a Thursday evenin.'

A stoat-up is the term used in football for the practice of restarting play with a dropped ball.

Anything excellent, but especially an attractive member of the opposite sex, may be called **a stoater**: 'He hit him a stoater right in the coupon.' 'That wis a big stoater ye nipped last night.'

Stoatin is used to mean two things: one is very good, as in 'That wis a stoatin dinner we hud roon at your place.' The other is stale, applied to food that has gone too hard to eat and would therefore be liable to bounce if dropped: 'If they scones are stoatin just pap them in the bin.'

A **stoat-the-baw** is a slang term for a paedophile, from the comparison of patting a child's head to bouncing a ball: 'Ah seen him in the Bar-L; he's a well-known stoat-the-baw.'

A **stoatybumper** is another slang term for anything excellent, being an amalgam of two other such words, *stoater* and *bumper.* 'Is this for me? Aw, ye're a wee stoatybumper, so ye are!'

stooky This Scots word for plaster, deriving from *stucco,* is used in various local expressions. A **stooky** is a plaster cast on a broken limb: 'Can Ah write ma name on yer stooky?' It is also used to mean a stupid or spiritless person, comparing them to a statue: 'Are you just gauny staun there like a stooky?'

To stooky a person (like **stiffen**) is to hit him extremely hard, especially to knock him unconscious: 'What did ye have tae go an stooky the guy for?'

stooshie An uproar or row: 'He's a popular guy an there'll be some stooshie if ye sack him.'

storm damage A local version of 'a few slates missing', i.e. an implication that someone is not right in the head: 'Ah wouldny pay too much attention to what he tells ye. There's a fair bit of storm damage there.'

Also used in adjectival form: 'C'moan oot a here. This guy's storm-damaged.'

stormer A slang term for anything considered outstandingly good: 'Mackay made sure of the points with an absolute stormer of a goal in the eighty-ninth minute.'

stotious (pronounced *stoe-shuss*) This is another word, probably an import from Ireland in this case, for drunk: 'Get him up tae his bed, he's stotious.'

stove To **stove in** or **get stoved in** means to partake of something enthusiastically: 'Help yersels tae champagne, lads, an get stoved inty they canapés.'

stowed (often pronounced to rhyme with *loud*) *or* **stowed-out** Full of people, crowded: 'We tried to get into the Scotia but it was stowed-out.'

striped face A graphic description of a face that bears scars: 'You wantin a striped face, pal? Well, shut it then.'

student tobacco A slang term for marijuana, arising from the alleged fondness for it of those involved in higher education, although its consumption is hardly exclusive to them: 'The wee brother hardly ever takes a drink. He's more inty the student tobacco, ye know?'

stupit-lookin An abusive adjective, popular among those who prefer not to swear: 'Gaun, ya stupit-lookin daft big clown, ye!'

sub A slang term for a boot: 'Ah wis sure Ah left ma subs under the bed.' **To sub** someone *or* **put the sub on** him is to kick him: 'It was a clean enough game till their sweeper put the sub on wee Charlie.'

sub crawl A kind of pub crawl that is exclusive to Glasgow, consisting of an attempt to travel round the Subway line, getting off at each of the fifteen stations and having a drink in the nearest pub before getting back on. Not recommended.

Subway Like New Yorkers, Glaswegians call the Underground railway **the Subway**. This reflects its original name, the Glasgow District Subway, and resists all official attempts to promote the term Underground: 'We'll get the Subway tae St Enoch an walk it fae there.'

Suckie A nickname for Sauchiehall Street: 'They stay up the far end a Suckie, near the Eye Infirmary.'

Sufferin General A waggish nickname for the Southern General Hospital: 'We'll take a run up an see yer granda in the Sufferin General.'

sugarollie-water A term applied by drinkers to any brew they consider insipid or over-sweet: 'How can ye drink sugarollie-water like this when they've got perfectly good export on draught?'

The literal meaning is a drink formerly made by children by shaking up pieces of sugarollie (liquorice) in a container of water.

sumdy A local pronunciation of *somebody*: 'Ah hink there sumdy at the door.'

supper No matter what the time of day, any dish sold at a chip-shop that consists of an item with chips is called a **supper**. Thus, a **pie supper** is a pie and chips, a **fish supper** is fish and chips, and so on: 'Run down tae Elio's an get us a pizza supper, two single fishes, three bars a choclit, an a big bottle a skoosh – any kind as long as it's diet.'

sure When someone wants someone else to confirm a statement he often frames a question using this: 'Sure it wis me that went for the papers yesterday, wasn't it?' 'It's no her that's tae get the first shot, sure it's no?'

swally (rhymes with *tally*) A local variant of *swallow*: 'Sumdy get a haud a that dug before it swallies the baw.' **The swally** is a slang term for alcoholic drink: 'He's too fond of the swally, that guy.' **A swally** means a drink or a drinking session: 'Who's for a wee swally the morra night?'

swatch (pronounced to rhyme with *match*) This means a look, especially a brief one, at something: 'Gie's another wee swatch at the instructions.'

sweary word An obscene or offensive word: 'Yer mammy'll no like that book. Too many sweary words in it.'

Sweaty Betty A legendary Glasgow female character troubled by problem perspiration: 'See this heat? Look at the oxters a this dress . . . Sweaty Betty's no in it!'

This lady is often accompanied by her equally mythical pal Hairy Mary.

swedger A slang word for a sweet: 'What gannet et aw the swedgers?'

sweeties The Scots word for confectionery turns up in several local expressions. Someone who feels he is underpaid in his job may complain of **working for sweeties.**

Similarly, low wages are often referred to as **sweetie-money**: 'Ye're workin for sweetie-money in here. Ye'd be better off on the Old King Cole.'

Someone who is very fond of confectionery can be labelled **sweetie-face**: 'Put the chocolates by before wee sweetie-face comes in.'

sweetie-wife The original meaning of this is a lady who keeps a sweet-shop, but it is often applied to any gossipy person, even a man: 'Ye canny get away fae him if he starts talkin tae ye, the aul sweetie-wife that he is.'

swimmies A familiar term for swimming gear: 'Don't forget yer swimmies the morra.'

swings A **shot on the swings** is a slang expression for the sexual act: 'Good weekend, was it? D'ye get a shot on the swings, aye?'

*Time that wean wis walkin.
She's a ton weight.*

taddie A familiar term for tadpole: 'Any jamjaurs, Maw? We're gaun fur taddies.'

tackety boots Hobnailed boots, studded with *tackets*: 'Aw the young lassies are gaun aboot wi big tackety boots on.'

tail The phrase **on your tail** means on your person, in your possession, and is usually used in referring to cash: 'Ah'm no gauny get very far wi wan-fifty oan ma tail, um Ah?'

take This verb is used in a local construction whereby people are not smitten by or afflicted with something undesirable but **take** it: 'The guy in front of me in the bus queue took a bad turn.' 'She hasny been ower the door since she took a bad back again.' 'If ye carry on like this ye'll take a heart attack.'

A not uncommon threat is **I'll take my hand off your jaw.** This means that the hand will rebound violently from your face, not that it has been lingering there already.

To **take in stairs** is to accept payment for washing other people's stairs in a tenement building, usually on the spot rather than, as the term might suggest, taking them away to do at home.

Tally A local term for Italian: 'The real Tally ice-cream's aye the nicest.' **Tally's blood** is a picturesque if rather old-fashioned nickname for the raspberry sauce often poured onto ice-cream cones.

tallyman A slang word for a moneylender or loanshark: 'Ah'm inty the tallyman fur a hunner.' Presumably the name comes from the moneylender keeping a tally of how much he is owed by whom.

tan To tan something is to use it up quickly ('We ferr tanned that hauf-boatle') or work briskly at it ('If we tan these last few orders we'll get away early the night').

    To tan a house is to burgle it: 'The polis says it's young boays that's tannin aw the hooses roon here.'

Tanics *or* **Tannies** Nicknames for the Botanic Gardens, in the West End: 'It wis a crackin day the day. The Tanics were full a punters sunbathin.'

tank **To tank** someone is to defeat him convincingly: 'We'll tank yeez in the next round.' **A tanking** is an example of this: 'Your lot took a right tankin yesterday.'

    To tank can also mean to move very fast, especially in a motor vehicle: 'Did ye see that fire engine tankin up the road a minute ago?'

    In slang use, one's **tank** can mean all the money one has on one: 'Ah've got a fiver an some smash, an that's ma tank.'

taste In a similar way to *smell*, this is used to mean taint, or give something a flavour of something else, usually undesirable: 'Don't leave that milk out while Ah'm paintin, or the paint'll taste it.'

tea If someone tells you **your tea's out**, if you're lucky this simply means a cup of tea has been poured for you or your evening meal has been served. Used in a metaphorical manner, the phrase means you are in trouble and should get ready to face the music: 'Yer tea's oot, pal. Ah'll get ye oot the back in two minutes.'

A **teaboy** is an insulting name to call someone who sucks up to a person in authority, implying that he slavishly fetches the tea for his master.

team A local term for a gang, as used in certain gang names like the Govan Team.

Team-handed means accompanied by several friends, especially when expecting trouble: 'Aye, ye're feart tae show yer face roon here unless ye come team-handit, ya crapbag, ye.'

tear (pronounced *terr*) This is a spree or any episode involving great enjoyment: 'Ye were havin a rerr wee terr tae yersel last night, weren't ye?'

Teddy Bears One of the nicknames for Rangers F. C. or their supporters. This was originally rhyming slang, playing on the local pronunciation of bears as *berrs,* which of course rhymes with *Gers.*

Teddy Bear Country is a nickname for the Ibrox area, home of Rangers' stadium, for those who want to go down to the woods: 'No way am Ah parkin a green motor overnight on a Saturday in Teddy Berr Country.'

Teenie Teenie fae Troon is a disparaging name applied to any female who presents a hoity-toity image or is much too fancily dressed for her surroundings: 'Wull ye look at Teenie fae Troon ower there! Where dis she think she is at aw?'

Teenie Leek is an affectionate name applied to a female child: 'Come on, Teenie Leek, time you were in your bed.'

ten-bob bit Ten bob (shillings) was the pre-decimal equivalent of 50p and is commemorated in this nickname for a fifty-pence piece: 'Ah need a twinty fur the meter an aw Ah've got's a ten-bob bit.'

ten-to-two feet Splayed feet, from the resemblance to the hands of a clock at this time: 'That's him there: the big stupit-lookin wan wi the ten-to-two feet.'

teuchter A mildly disparaging term for a Highlander: 'Her aul man's a teuchter.' 'Ye canny miss that big red teuchter face of his.'

that's A strange, and somewhat redundant, local use of the possessive: 'That's mines, but whose is that's?'

there Like *here* this is often used on its own where a verb would normally follow: 'There a big wasp in the lavvy.' 'There ma taxi noo.' 'There only the two of us comin.'

thingmy, thingmyjig, thingwy These words are used as substitutes for the proper names, temporarily forgotten, of something or someone: 'Ah got wee Mrs Thingmy up the road.' 'Gie's another a they thingwies.'

this is me Not a redundant introduction of oneself, but part of a description of one's circumstances: 'This is me since yesterday, nuthin tae eat.' 'Ah canny shift this cold at aw. This is me loaded fae last Tuesday.'

Thistle, the A nickname for Partick Thistle F. C.: 'Fancy gaun tae the Thistle game for a wee change?'

thorn A slang word, particularly in the building trade, for a nail: 'See's ower a handful a thorns, will ye?'

thought A thought is used to mean anything unpleasant or requiring real force of will to face or accomplish: 'It's a thought havin to go back to that big empty house on my own.'

'Tic, the A nickname for Celtic F. C., handy for headline-writers on the sports pages: ''TIC RAP REF.'

ticket A slang word for a person. A **hard ticket** is someone who acts or looks tough: 'Ah wouldny argue wi a hard ticket like that.' A **useless ticket** is a person considered as good for nothing or shiftless: 'He lies in his bed hauf the day, the useless ticket!'

tim To tim a container, especially one holding liquid, is to empty it: 'Tim thae cups inty the sink, will ye?' 'He timt the hale boatle doon the stank.'

Tim A nickname for a Roman Catholic, apparently shortened from *Tim Malloy*, although whether this was an actual individual or a kind of generic name I have not been able to discover: 'She married a Tim, your sister, didn't she?'

A chapel is sometimes referred to as a **Timshop.**

toe-ender A kick, using the point of the boot: 'You call it a well-placed shot an I say it was nothin but a jammy toe-ender.' 'Get oot ma road or ye'll get a toe-ender.'

toley A local word for the product of a bowel movement. Like many such terms it is often used as a name to call someone objectionable.

ton weight A term applied to anything, including people, considered to be very heavy: 'Time that wean wis walkin. She's a ton weight.'

tore Someone who energetically sets about a person or thing is often said to **get tore in**: 'Ah'm gaun roon there this minute tae get tore inty the bampot.' 'Get tore right inty they samosas afore they get cauld.'

torn-faced A term applied to someone who looks miserable or aggrieved, especially if this is his habitual expression: 'That social worker Ah had tae see was a right torn-faced bisom.'

toss *or* **tossbag** An insulting name: 'Whit're *you* sayin, ya toss?' The suggestion is that the person insulted is given to self-abuse.

tosser Most often found in the phrase **not worth a tosser**, this means a coin of low value, such as a penny used in games of pitch and toss: 'That video you selt us isny worth a tosser.' 'Ah don't care a tosser what you think.'

tother **Nae tother** means no trouble: 'We'll get this finished this mornin nae tother.' This is shortened from *nae tother a baw*, which is a deliberately spoonerised version of *nae bother at aw*.

totty A local word for a potato: 'Gie's a baked totty an chili.'

To say that someone is **no the clean totty** is to suggest that he is involved in dishonest activities. Presumably this is a comparison to a potato that still has dirt sticking to it.

A **totty-peelin** accent or voice is one considered posh or affected: 'She jist puts on that totty-peelin voice when she answers the phone.'

A **totty scone** is the local term for a potato scone: 'Ah'll just have one of your totty scones cold, wi a wee bit butter on it.'

A woman wearing clothes that emphasise her plumpness is often compared to a **bag of totties**: 'Ah'm lik a bag a totties in this dress noo.'

toty A term applied to anything very small or a person very young: 'Aw! Look at these wee toty shoes.' 'Ye said he wisny tall but ye never said he wis toty!'

trackie A tracksuit: 'Kin Ah get a Scotland trackie fur ma Christmas?'

Trackie bottoms are the lower half of a tracksuit, adopted as casual wear for all occasions: 'Mammy! She's away oot in ma trackie bottoms an she never even asked us!'

trainies A local term for training shoes: 'The boay wants forty quid for a new pair a trainies!'

troubles Someone who is beset by difficulties may have it said of him that he **doesn't have his troubles to seek**: 'She's no got her troubles tae seek since she got mixed up wi that useless ticket.'

trouble-the-hoose A title given to a young baby whose crying and urgent needs inevitably disturb the peace of the household: 'See's ower wee Trouble-the-hoose till you get a cuppa tea.'

tube A stupid or contemptible person: 'Yer bum's out the windy, ya tube, ye!'

tummle Tumble. To **tummle yer wilkies** is to do a somersault: 'Wait till ye see the wean tummlin his wilkies.' This apparently comes from the idea of tumbling like wildcats.

To **take a tummle to** oneself is to see the error of one's ways, smarten up one's thinking or behaviour: 'You better take a tummle tae yersel or ye'll be gettin yer jotters.'

tumshie A turnip. The word is often used as an insult implying stupidity: 'How'd ye expect the kettle tae boil when it's no even plugged in, ya tumshie?' A stupid person may also be referred to as **tumshie-heid.**

tuppence Two pence in pre-decimal money, but still heard in popular idioms. A small child may be described as being **no the size a tuppence.**

No worth tuppence can mean that a thing is of little value, or, when applied to people, that someone is exhausted: 'Ah'm no worth tuppence efter Ah've come up they stairs.'

turkey Someone who eats a great deal at a sitting may be said to **stuff his turkey**: 'D'ye mean tae say you've been sittin here stuffin yer turkey while I've been out graftin?'

turn A **turn** is a win at gambling, perhaps reflecting the punter's necessary faith that everyone gets a chance to be lucky: 'Ah see Joe's had a turn. Away an nip him for a blue job.'

twally (rhymes with *Sally*) An idiot: 'Ah said no tae drap your end till Ah telt ye, ya twally!'

twicet A local form of *twice*: 'She's been wanst an Ah've been twicet.'

two-up The **two-up** is the offensive V-sign made with two fingers: 'Dae you let yer wee boay away wi giein folk the two-up?'

Ye jist cannae be up tae um!

um In broad Glaswegian speech, a version of *him*: 'If Ah get um Ah'm gauny stiffen um.'

Uni Short for University, of which Glasgow now has more than it used to. **The Uni** tends to mean the University of Glasgow in particular: 'He's managed to get a flat up near the Uni.'

up In the field of gambling, to describe something as **up** means that it has won: 'Maybe we'll have the coupon up this week.' 'That's me got a line up.'

    The phrase **up the toon** means into the city centre: 'Ah'm away up the toon fur a new jaiket.'

    Ye canny be up tae um is said of someone, especially a mischievous child, whose behaviour is impossible to predict: 'Ah sent um inty the hoose cause he wis pullin up ma daffadils, an when Ah went in he wis feedin the baby a dug biscuit . . . ye just canny be up tae um!'

ur A local version of *are*: 'Ye're a great wee soul, so ye ur!'

urny The negative of the above, *aren't*: 'Ye urny much good at this, ur ye?' 'We urny gettin away early at aw.'

160

He used tae work in Pearson's in Vicky Road, feedin the parrot...

verse This means to play against someone in a game: 'Away in an get yer baw an Ah'll verse ye at heidies.' This odd expression comes from the term *versus* (as in Pollok versus Rob Roy) being understood as if it was a verb *verses*.

vicky The **vicky** is the rude two-fingered V-sign: 'He got sent off for givin the fans the vicky.' The term is probably shortened from *victory*, as in the V-sign popularised during the Second World War by Winston Churchill.

Vicky, the A familiar name for the Victoria Infirmary: 'She's got that much wrong with her she's got a season ticket for the Vicky.'

Vicky Road A familiar name for Victoria Road, a main business and shopping thoroughfare on the South Side: 'He used tae work in Pearson's in Vicky Road, feedin the parrot.'

voddy Vodka: 'She's tanned a hale boatle a voddy hersel.' 'Gie's two voddies . . . wan wi lime in it.'

Right intae the wid...

waccy baccy A slang term for marijuana: 'What are you gigglin at? Been at the waccy baccy or somethin?'

wae In broad Glaswegian speech, a version of *with*: 'If yeez ur aw gaun Ah'm comin wae yeez.'

Walk, the The name by which most people refer to the Orange Walk, held each year on the Saturday nearest to the twelfth of July: 'We were held up for ages with the Walk goin' along the Paisley Road.'

To **break the Walk** is to cross the street in front of the main body of the parade or through a gap between bands; not recommended to endear one to the marchers.

There are other minor Orange marches in the summer, before the main one, and these are known as **wee walks.**

wallies (pronounced to rhyme with *valleys*) This means false teeth: 'If Ah've tae spend any mair on fillins Ah'm gauny get that dentist tae rip the hale jing-bang oot an gie us a set a wallies.' The term suggests that the false teeth might be made of china, or *wally*.

Wallies is also a collective term for a very small sum of money, especially poor wages: 'Ye get paid wallies in that place.' The origin of this might be the former childhood use of bits of broken china as play-money.

walloper A slang term for the penis.

wally (rhyming with *valley*) This means made from china or porcelain. A **wally dug** is an ornament in the form of a china dog: 'Look at the two of them sittin at both ends of the settee like a pair a wally dugs.'

A **wally close** is a close in a tenement building that has china tiles on its walls rather than just paint, considered a sign of poshness: 'That last flat we looked at was the best . . . a wally close an aw!'

The **wally waw,** literally porcelain wall, is a slang term for a gents' urinal of the kind consisting of one complete porcelain receptacle running the length of a wall: 'Ach well, Ah'll need tae go an staun at the wally waw.'

Someone who is described as having a **wally heid** is considered simple-minded, not right in the head. Similarly, to call someone **wally-heid** shows that you think he is a simpleton.

wan A local term for *one*: 'At wan's mines.' 'Ah'll get ye at hauf wan.'

wance Once: 'Ah only went the wance.'

wanner *or* **wanny** To do something **in a wanner** *or* **wanny** is to do it in one: 'He horsed back his lager in a wanner.'

To wanner a person is to give him a single destructive punch: 'Wee Eddie just walked right up tae the guy an wannered um.'

wanst A local term for *once*: 'Wanst I had a secret lo-ove . . .'

wap (rhymes with *cap*) A multipurpose word, somewhat onomatopoeic. It can mean to hit: 'She wapped him wan ower the heid.' Or a blow: 'It's only a bluebottle . . . gie it a wap wi the paper.' It can also be a sound effect: 'Ah beltit roon the coarner – wap! – right inty this big bear!'

warmer (sometimes pronounced to rhyme with *farmer*) This is a word for an exasperating or despicable person: 'He wouldny gie the weans their baw back when it went inty his garden, the aul warmer that he is!'

washers (pronounced to rhyme with *rashers*) This is a disparaging term for small change: 'When Ah asked ye fur change of a pound Ah wis hopin fur two fifties, no a pile a washers.'

waste **To waste** a thing or a person is to spoil it: 'Don't let the dug jump up on the new settee or she'll waste it.' To **waste someone's face** is to disfigure it by violence: 'If he comes that crack wi me Ah'll waste his face for him.'

A **wastit** person, especially a child, is someone who has been spoiled by being over-indulged: 'Weans nooadays are wastit wi aw their videos an CD-ROMS an aw that.' 'Can you no act lik a grown man instead of a big wastit wean?' A person who looks sulky may be called **wastit-face.**

Someone whose **heid's wastit** is stupid, distracted, or simply too tired to think properly: 'Never mind askin that big stumer . . . . . . his heid's wastit.' 'Ah'm tryin tae think of a phone number but ma heid's wastit after the day Ah've had.'

watchie A familiar term for a watchman: 'Ye'd think the watchie would check they weans for playin on that site.'

watter Water. To go **doon the watter** is a traditional Glasgow phrase which means to take a pleasure-cruise down the river and Firth of Clyde to various resorts such as Millport, Rothesay or Largs.

wauchle Someone who **wauchles** walks in a shuffling or waddling manner: 'Ye see that aul bloke wauchlin roon for his paper every mornin in life.'

way **On yer way!** is of course a phrase used to tell someone to leave, but in some contexts, such as at a football game, it can be a cry of encouragement: 'On yer way, big yin! Take the lot a them on yersel!'

wean (pronounced *wayne*) The local term, as opposed to the more easterly *bairn*, for a baby or child: 'Ah'll need to go an get the weans from school.' 'She's another wean on the road.' A **big wean** is a grown-up who is acting childishly: 'He's gauny start greetin in a minute, the big wean.'

weather The phrase **this weather** is used to mean at this time or these days: 'How's yer aul faither keepin this weather?'

wee The Scots word for *small* is used to mean younger: 'Ma wee brother an ma wee cousin are comin round.'
   Wee-er means smaller or younger: 'Ye need a wee-er screw than that.' 'It's only the wee-er weans that are gettin oot early.'
   Wee-est means smallest or youngest: 'Who's the wee-est at your Brownies?'

wee boy A term used to mean a particular individual, especially one who is ideally suited for a specific task: 'That guy needs to be told to mind his own business, an I'm the wee boy to do it!'

wee goldie A familiar name for a glass of whisky, alluding to the drink's golden colour: 'Stick a wee goldie for auld Walter on the round next time.'

wee man An affectionate title or form of address for a small individual: 'Wantin a run up the road, wee man?' **In the name a the wee man!** is a cry of surprise, disgust or astonishment: 'In the name a the wee man! Wid ye look at the state a them!' Apparently the particular wee man referred to was originally the Devil.
   A **wee man** is often used to mean a tradesman employed to do specific jobs, irrespective of his actual stature: 'My mother says she'll get a wee man out the local paper to do the garden.'

wee team A familiar term for the reserve team of a football club, the **big team** being the first team: 'The big no-user canny even get a game for the wee team.'

well Used in the sense of 'in that case', this turns up at the end rather than the beginning of statements: 'Are ye no wantin that tottie? Gie it tae me, well.'

well-fired Describes baked items, like rolls, loaves, or scones, that have been in the oven longer than others and are almost black on the outside: 'Ye know yer granda likes a well-fired roll in the mornin.'

well-got A local variant of *well in*, being on good terms with: 'Aye, he gets aw the overtime he wants cause he's well-got wi that supervisor.'

wellied Another term meaning *drunk*: 'He was that wellied he disny even mind me talkin tae him.'
   To **get wellied in** means the same as get stuck in, that is, to set about something vigorously: 'Right, boys, let's get wellied inty this carry-out.'

well on In an advanced state of inebriation: 'Wan look at her an ye could see she was well on already.'

well seen Plain, patently obvious, to be expected: 'There was some queue for petrol. It's well seen there's a Budget today.'

welly As a verb this means to kick powerfully: 'Celtic areny a team tae just welly it up the park an chase it.'

went Used where others would say *gone*: 'He hasny went back since.' If someone says 'The door went' this doesn't mean that it has independently parted company with its hinges and disappeared but that there was a knock or ring at the door. The same applies to telephones, bells, sirens etc.: 'We'll make it. The bell hasny went yet.'

West-Endie An inhabitant of Glasgow's West End, an area roughly west of Charing Cross, north of Argyle Street, south of Maryhill Road, and shading away westwards to the far suburbs. This is its geography, but some would say it is more a state of mind. It is the famous stamping ground of students (real and pretend ones), artists (ditto) and fashionables. The fuller

166

form of the term, **trendy West-Endie**, gives an idea of how this sub-culture is viewed in other parts of the city: 'This used tae be a real workin-man's pub. Noo it's full a West-Endies an heid-the-baws makin documentaries.'

Western, the To say that someone is 'in the Western' is not to imply a role in a cowboy film but that the individual concerned is a patient in the Western Infirmary.

whack The phrase **not the full whack** means incomplete, not up to scratch, below par: 'Are you feelin okay? Ye're not lookin the full whack today at all.'

For **cop your whack** see under **cop**.

what The phrase **what is it?** is a common way of asking someone what he would like to drink. Another similar question is **what are you on?** which can also (when emphasis is put on *on*) be an implication that the person addressed has done something so ridiculous that he must be drunk or high on drugs: 'Ye did what? What are you *on*, pal?'

Whatevery's A local nickname for any branch of What Everyone Wants, a chain of inexpensive clothes shops: 'She says she got the exact same coat oot Whatevery's fur hauf the price.'

wheech (pronounced with the *ch* as in *loch*) This means to move (or move a thing) away at great speed: 'We'll jump in the motor an wheech down to Largs for the day.' 'Ah'd just taken wan bite oot ma piece an put it doon for minute when that dampt dug came up an wheeched it.'

wheesht To **haud yer wheesht** means to keep quiet, refrain from talking: 'Would youse lot haud yer wheesht till we hear what the man's sayin?' **Wheesht!** is a command to be silent.

whitey *or* **white-oot** To **take a whitey** *or* **white-oot** means to suddenly turn pale because of feeling sick or dizzy: 'See that boay takin a whitey? Get him oot inty the close away fae ma good carpet.'

wick A **wick** is an annoying or bad-natured person: 'Leave yer wee brither alane, ya wee wick, ye.'

wid[1] A local variant of *would*: 'Wid ye credit it?' The negative of this is **widny**: 'Ah widny dae that tae emdy.'

wid[2] A local variant of *wood*: 'Ah canny go that French bread . . . it's lik chowin a dod a wid.'

Someone who has had a very short haircut may have it decribed as **right inty the wid.**

Widden means made of wood, wooden: 'Ye're better wi an iron gate than a widden wan.'

wide To **make someone wide** is to let him in on some useful information, put him wise to the facts: 'Ah knew this wis comin aff. Big Dan made us wide tae it the other night.'

A **wide member** is a flyman (see **wido**).

wido *or* **wide-oh** A slang term for a rogue, criminal or flyman: 'The only folk that drink in here are neds, chancers, hardmen, an widos. Whit wan are you?'

wilkies For **tummle yer wilkies** see under **tummle.**

willn't, willny Two local versions of *will not* or *won't*: 'He says he'll come but I know he willn't.'

Wilma A nickname for a female Protestant, especially a Rangers supporter, being a feminine form of *William*.

winch To **winch** is to kiss and cuddle: 'They were winchin in the back row at the pictures.' It also means to go out regularly with someone of the opposite sex, to date him or her: 'The pair a them've been winchin for ages.' The question 'Are ye winchin?' is often asked of young people by their elders who wish to embarrass them, meaning 'Are you going out with someone?'

windy *or* **windae** A local word for *window*: 'Shut that windae or the budgie'll be aff its mark.'

If something is described as **out the windy** this means it is no longer possible: 'We were gauny get a new fittit kitchen till he lost his job an that was that oot the windy.'

Yer bum's out the windy means 'You are talking nonsense.' I suppose the suggestion is that what you are saying is so outrageously silly that you should be as embarrassed to be heard saying it as you would be if you were making a public exhibition of your posterior.

Wine City A disparaging nickname for the Greenock/Port Glasgow conurbation, deriving from the Glaswegian belief that the natives thereof yield to no others as champion consumers of cheap strong wine.

wine-mopper A disparaging term for someone who drinks fortified cheap wine, especially a down-and-out: 'You're gauny end up sleepin on Glesga Green wi the rest a the wine-moppers.' It is sometimes shortened to **mopper.**

wineshop A slang term for a pub that specialises in selling cheap strong wine by the glass: 'Naw, we don't stock that in here. It's a wineshop you're wantin, aul yin, no a wine bar.'

wired If a person is described as **wired up but no plugged in** this means he is not right in the head.
   An individual who is slightly crazy or abnormally energetic may be described as being **wired to the moon.** Another version of this is **wired to a Mars Bar.**

wise A person described as being **not wise** *or* **no wise** is considered gullible: 'Ye canny be expected tae agree tae that . . . d'ye want people tae think ye're no wise?'

wiss A slang term for urination: 'Ah'll just dive in fur a wiss.'

workie A familiar term for a workman: 'There's a gang a workies diggin up the street.'

worky up In children's talk this means to get your swing going from a standing start up to the speed and height of arc desired: 'You sit on the swing next to me an I'll show ye how to worky up.'

wrap it To stop doing something, cancel something: 'If Ah don't win somethin on the lottery soon Ah'm fur wrappin it.' 'When he said it would take another three weeks for delivery I told him just to wrap the whole thing.'

Wrap it! is also used to command someone to stop talking.

wrecked A slang term for extremely tired, exhausted: 'They only got halfway up Ben Lomond and that was them wrecked.'

wulk A whelk. **To howk one's wulk** is to pick one's nose, presumably comparing this activity to prising a whelk out of its shell.

Full as a wulk is another term for drunk, implying, I suppose, that the person so described can no sooner swallow any more drink than a shell with a whelk in it can contain anything else.

wulln't, wullny Broad Glaswegian pronunciations of *willn't* and *willny*: 'The wean wullny eat chicken.'

wummin A woman: 'There a picture of a big bare wummin on the front a that video.'

Mrs Wummin is a name used to address or refer to a woman who is unknown to the speaker; 'Haw! Mrs Wummin! It's you next.'

wur A broad Glaswegian term for *our*: 'Where ur we gaun wur hoalidays this year?'

wursels Ourselves: 'Jist when we're beginnin tae enjoy wursels we've tae go hame.'

X, Y &

Big zeds.

-y The word *of* in broad Glasgow speech often comes out sounding like a *y* added to the end of the word it follows: 'Gie us somey they crisps.' 'Ah'm fed up wi the pairy yeez.'

ya bass An expression originally found in gang slogans marked on walls, as in 'Pollok Crew ya bass', which I assume is a punchier version of 'you bastard'. The phrase crossed over into more common use as part of any bombastic and defiant statement: 'Govan Initiative rule, ya bass!'

yabber To talk idly, chatter: 'Ah canny concentrate on ma crossword wi aw yer yabberin.'

yap An extremely talkative or gossipy person: 'That wee yap would talk the hind legs off a donkey.'

ye A form of *you* which is often appended to an insult, magnifying and focussing its strength: 'Ya stupit-lookin monkey, ye!'
   The plural form is **yeez**: 'If ye think yeez are onty a cushy number here yeez've got another think comin.'

yelp A term for a child that is continually whingeing or being cheeky: 'An that lassie a theirs is a right wee yelp an aw.'

yin A form of *one* that in Glasgow speech is only used as an object of a statement: 'Ah'll have that yin there.' It is often used to refer to people, particularly in tandem with an adjective describing the person: **auld yin, big yin, wee yin, young yin.**

The plural is **yins**: 'These yins are the best.' It often turns up in combinations, referring to people as a group: **them yins, youse yins, us yins**.

yon time A term used to mean an undetermined but far too late hour: 'Are we expected to hang around this place till yon time?'

yop School slang for clype, tell on someone: 'Ah hink Ah know who yopped on us.' Someone who does this is **a yop** *or* **yopper.**

yous Used to address more than one person at the same time: 'Any a yous got a light?'

y's A slang term for male underpants: 'Ah canny find a clean pair a y's.'

yuck it A Glasgow variation of *chuck it*, that is, stop it: 'Yuck it, yous or Ah'm tellin on yeez.'

yumyum A cake highly popular in Glasgow, whose citizens of course yield to no-one in the field of teeth-destroying sweet things. For those who don't know, it is similar in consistency to a doughnut, but is oblong rather than round and is sometimes twisted in the middle: 'Ah canny make ma mind up between yumyums an empire biscuits.'

zed To **have a few zeds** and **stack up some zeds** are slang expressions meaning to have a sleep. **Big zeds** means a long deep sleep, as opposed to forty winks: 'Ah'm definitely needin big zeds the night. Ma eyes are hingin oot ma heid.'

The origin of this is the children's comics convention of showing that a character is asleep by inserting a string of zeds where a speech bubble would normally go.

Rhyming slang

A lot of rhyming slang is used in everyday Glasgow speech, not all of which was coined there. In this compilation I have tried to include only examples that are genuinely Glaswegian in origin, even though some of them have gone on to achieve a wider currency.

One of the factors that make rhyming slang unintelligible to the uninitiated is that individual expressions often consist of two words, the second part, which gives the rhyme, often being unspoken but understood by hearers who are in the know. Because of this I list my items in alphabetical order according to the first word, in the hope that a reader will find the meaning of an expression suspected to be rhyming slang even if only the first part has been heard.

Abraham Lincoln Stinkin: 'Your plates are Abraham Lincoln!'

acme wringers Fingers. The fact that this rhymes is an illustration of the local pronunciation of fingers. An Acme Wringer I assume to be a proprietary brand of clothes wringer.

Arthur Lowe No, a negative answer: 'Fancy another?' 'Ah widny say arthur.' The late Arthur Lowe was, of course, a household name as the star of several popular TV comedy series of the 1970s, such as *Dad's Army*.

Bayne and Ducket A bucket, using the name of a well-known chain of shoe shops. Sometimes used as an exclamation, substituting for something a good deal stronger.

Bengal Lancer A chancer: 'Whit's that big Bengal sayin noo?'

Bob Hope Dope, i.e. marijuana: 'Fancy a blast a the old Bob?'

Carolina China, meaning a friend. This is an example of one piece of rhyming slang standing for another, as *china* itself is also rhyming slang (china plate = mate).

Chic Murray The late and much lamented droll comedian's name is taken in vain for a curry. Some people prefer to use **Ruby Murray.**

corned beef Deef, i.e. deaf: 'Ye'll need tae speak up a bit, son; Ah'm a wee bit corned beef.' Sometimes shortened to **corny.**

Cowdenbeath Teeth: 'Ah'll just run the brush roon the aul Cowdenbeath then Ah'm inty ma scratcher.'

cream bun Hun, i.e. a Protestant.

cream cookie A bookie, including his premises or betting shop: 'Away doon the cream cookie an lift whit's lyin for this line.'

cream puff Huff: 'He's no talkin tae us noo . . . he's took the cream puff.'

Crossmyloof Poof, i.e. male homosexual. Crossmyloof is an area of the South Side formerly famous for its skating rink.

currant bun A nun.

Dan Dares Flares, i.e. flared trousers. After the spaceman hero of the *Eagle* comic: 'Ah see the Dan Dares are comin back inty fashion.'

deedle doddle Model, i.e. Model Lodging House (see **model** in main text): 'Guess who Ah seen gaun inty the deedle doddle?'

dirty beast A priest.

disco dancer Chancer: 'He's a bitty a disco dancer that pal a yours, eh?'

dolly dimple Simple, in the sense of not very clever: 'Ye'll need tae excuse her . . . she's a wee bit dolly.'

Donald Duck Luck. Often shortened to **donald**: 'If there's nae tickets left when ye get there it's just yer donald.'

Duke of Argylls Piles; haemorrhoids, that is: 'He's a martyr tae the Duke of Argylls, so he is.'

Duke of Montrose Nose.

Easter egg Beg, as in **on the Easter egg,** begging for money: 'Never mind comin roon here on the Easter egg, ya aul moocher, ye.'

Elsie Tanner A wanner, i.e. a single complete example or action: 'Whit d'ye hink? Another coat a emulsion on the ceilin or lee it wi an Elsie Tanner?' This derives from the name of a well-known former character in the TV soap opera *Coronation Street.*

everlastin joob-joob A tube, i.e. the slang word for an idiot: 'Look at the mess ye're makin, ya everlastin joob-joob.' The term literally means a kind of long-lasting sucking sweetie.

Friar Tucked Thwarted.

Garngad (an area in the north-east of the city) Bad: 'How ye gettin on the day?' 'No too Garngad.' This reflects the local pronunciation which accents the second syllable.

gas-cookered Snookered, i.e. thwarted, prevented from getting something done: 'If that last nut'll no shift that'll be us gas-cookered.'

gasket jint (*jint* being a local pronunciation of *joint,* on the model of *jiner,* joiner) Pint, usually of beer: 'Moan we'll nick oot fur a couple a gaskets.'

Gene Tunney Money. This one shows its age when you know that Gene Tunney was an American boxer who was world heavyweight champion 1926–28.

gone an dunnit Bunnit: 'Now where did I put ma gone an dunnit?'

good looks Books, in the sense of the employment documents returned to a sacked worker: 'Carry on like this an ye'll be gettin yer good looks.'

Gregory Pecks Specs, meaning spectacles, glasses: 'Time Ah wis gettin testit fur a new pair a Gregories.'

Hampden Roar Score, as used in the question 'What's the score?' meaning what's going on, what's the story: 'What's the Hampden Roar wi aw this shoutin an bawlin?'

ham sandwich Language. This only works if you remember that the second part is often pronounced as *sangwidge*. 'Just keep the ham sangwidge respectable in front a ma aul dear, eh?'

harry hoof Poof, i.e. male homosexual.

Harry Wraggs Jags, which is, of course, a nickname for Partick Thistle F. C.: 'We're the Jags, Harry Wraggs!' The individual whose name is borrowed here was a famous racing jockey and trainer in the 1930s.

haw maw In the singular this can mean a saw: 'See's ower the big haw maw.' In the plural it means baws, i.e. testicles: 'Ooyah, right in the haw maws!' 'Ye've made a right haw maws a this.'
  The expression **haw maw** itself is a cry to attract the attention of one's mother.

hey-diddle-diddle Fiddle, in the sense of a swindle: 'He was caught at the hey-diddle-diddle with the books.'

hi-diddler Fiddler, i.e. violin player: 'There's a hi-diddler giein it laldy in the lounge.'

hillbilly Chilly: 'Ah thought it was gauny be nice this mornin but it's turned kinna hillbilly noo.'

holy ghost Coast: 'Fancy a wee run doon the holy ghost?'

honey perrs Sterrs, i.e. stairs: 'Ah'm away up the honey perrs.' **Honey perrs!** meaning sweet pears, was an old street cry of a fruit-seller.

hoosie Fraser House of Fraser, the department-store company, used here to mean razor. Sometimes shortened to **hoosie** (rhymes with *Lucy*).

hot peas Knees.

iron lung Bung, i.e. a tip or gratuity: 'The moolly aul get never even gied us an iron lung.'

Jack and Jill The Pill: 'She's wantin tae come aff the Jack.'

Jack Dash A slash, i.e. urination: 'Ah'll just have a quick Jack Dash then we're off.'

jaggy nettle Kettle: 'Stick the jaggy on for a coffee.'

jeely jar Car: 'Is this the new jeely jar, eh?'

Jock Mackay A pie, usually taken to mean a Scotch pie: 'Ah had a couple a Jock Mackays fur ma tea.' This mythical person also turns up in an expression said as a sigh: 'Och aye, Jock Mackay.'

Joe Baxi A taxi: 'Never mind the motor. We'll dive inty a Joe Baxi.'

Joe the toff Off, i.e. away, gone, on one's way: 'Right, that's me Joe the toff. Cheerybyes!'

John Greigs Legs: 'A fine pair a John Greigs.' The man referred to is, of course, a famous Rangers player of the '60s and '70s.

Jungle Jim Tim, i.e. a Roman Catholic: 'Just cause ye've got an Irish name doesny mean ye're a Jungle Jim.'

kelly bow Dough, i.e. money: 'Ah'd get ye a pint but Ah'm kinna light on the kelly bow at the moment.'

Kenneth Mackellar Cellar.

Legal Aid Lemonade: 'A wee splash a the Legal Aid in wan a they haufs, young yin.'

lemon curd Burd (bird), i.e. a young woman, especially one's girlfriend: 'Canny make it the night. It's the lemon curd's birthday.'

Lilian Gish Pish: 'Ah got caught short for a Lilian Gish.'

Similarly, **Lilian Gished** means pished, i.e. drunk. What a way to commemorate a movie star!

love an romancin Dancin: 'Ma folks are away tae the love an romancin at the Plaza.'

Macnamara Barra, i.e. barrow: 'Gie us a haun tae load these bricks inty the Macnamara, wull ye?'

mammy mine Wine: 'He's a wee bit too fond a the mammy mine.'

Manfred Mann Tan, as in suntan: 'She's away doon tae the sunbed tae top up the Manfred Mann.'

man from Cairo A giro, i.e. benefits payment.

Mars Bar Scar: 'You're lookin for a Mars Bar, pal.'

merry laird Beard (in local pronunciation, *baird* or *berrd*): 'What made ye decide to get rid of the merry laird?'

Mickey Mouse Grouse, i.e. a measure of the famous proprietary brand of whisky: 'A Mickey Mouse an a wee heavy, barman.'

Mickey Rooney Loony, i.e. an insane person: 'It's no joke stayin through the waw fae a Mickey Rooney lik that.'

Mick Jagger Lager: 'They Mick Jaggers in the fridge should be nice an cauld now.' This only constitutes a rhyme in local pronunciation. In London, for example, *Jagger* and *lager* have different sounds.

Mr Happy A nappy: 'It's definitely your turn to change the wee guy's Mr Happy.' This of course refers to the smiling symbol of the 'Glasgow's Miles Better' campaign.

Moby Dick Sick: 'Haud on a minute, Ah'm feelin a bit Moby.'

mountain goat Coat: 'Ah'm pittin oan the mountain goat, case it gets hillbilly later on.'

Oscar Slater Later: 'Ah'll get ye Oscar Slater.' The name comes from the defendant in a highly controversial murder case in Glasgow.

178

Paddy McGuigan Jiggin, i.e. dancing: 'We're aw gaun tae the Paddy McGuigan the night.' I take this to refer to a supposedly typical Irish name rather than to any particular individual.

Paddy McGuire A fire: 'Sling another shovel on the Paddy McGuire while ye're up.' The comment on the preceding name also applies here.

pan breid Deid, i.e. dead: 'Ye never telt us yer dug wis pan breid.'

Pansy Potters Jotters, i.e. cards or what one gets when one is dismissed from employment: 'She'd only been there a year when they gave her her Pansy Potters.'

paraffin ile (*ile* being a local pronunciation of *oil*) Style: 'Ye never see Wee Jack gaun oot withoot a bit a paraffin ile aboot him.'

Parkheid smiddies Diddies, i.e. a woman's breasts. This comes from a famous forge in Parkhead, in the city's East End.

Pat and Mick Sick: 'He's huvin a couple a days aff oan the Pat an Mick.'

pea pod Tod. **On yer pea pod** means **on yer tod**, which means on your own, alone. Like *Carolina*, this is a case of one piece of rhyming slang standing for another, as *tod* is short for Tod Sloan and **on yer Tod Sloan** is rhyming slang for on your own: 'Are you gauny let her walk up the road on her pea pod?'

pearl diver A fiver, i.e. a five-pound note: 'Ah fun a pearl diver doon the settee.'

pineapple Chapel. The stress of the pronunciation goes on the second part of the word, i.e. pine*apple*: 'Yer mammy's away up at the pineapple.'

pot of glue Clue: 'He hasny got a pot, the stumer that he is.'

pottit heid Deid, i.e. deceased: 'Ah think yer goldfish is pottit heid.'

Potted head is, of course, a traditional Scots delicacy.

radio rental Mental, i.e. insane: 'The guy's totally radio, Ah'm tellin ye.'

rooty-ma-toot A suit: 'Should Ah put on the rooty-ma-toot for this do?'

Rory O'More Door: 'Hey! Gauny shut the Rory O'More, there's a hell ae a George Raft.'

Rossy Docks Socks: 'Ah'm huntin fur a clean pair a Rossy Docks.' **Rossy** is of course a local pronunciation of *Rothesay*.

Ruby Murray A curry. The lady in question was a well-known singer.

St Louis blues News: 'Bung the telly on till we get the St Louis blues.'

satin and silk Milk: 'We'll have a cup a tea when the wean comes back wi the satin an silk.'

scooby doo Clue. See **scooby** in main text.

single fish Pish: 'Ah'll need tae go for a single fish.' 'Well, get us a pie supper.'

skin diver A fiver.

soapy bubble Trouble: 'Tell yer mate he's in deep soapy.'

song an dancer Chancer: 'Ah hear the new boyfriend's a bit of a song an dancer.'

south of the border Out of order, meaning unacceptable, not the done thing in terms of behaviour: 'Here, is that no a wee bit south of the border whit he's sayin?'
   The border referred to is that between the United States and Mexico, rather than Scotland and England, an example of the Glaswegian love for and identification with the Western movie.

tackety bits (literally hobnailed boots) Tits. Often shortened to **tacketies**: 'That's a fine perr a tacketies on that wee thing.'

taury (i.e. tarry) **rope** The Pope: 'When wis it the aul taury rope wis at Bellahouston Park?'

teedle-ee A pee, i.e. urination: 'He'll no be long. He's just away for a teedle-ee.' I would take this as coming from deedling, that is, singing meaningless words in imitation of music played by a band.

tin flute A suit: 'Ye better wear the tin flute for yer interview.'

Tommy Trotter A snotter: 'Ye've a wee Tommy Trotter at yer nose.'
   I don't know if this refers to an actual person, but if so he must have been fairly unpleasant to be thus commemorated.

varicose veins Weans.

wine grape Pape, i.e. a Roman Catholic: 'It's aw wine grapes that drink in there.'

winners and losers Troosers, i.e. trousers: 'Haud on till Ah put ma galluses on these winners an losers.'

Rhyming slang for first names

A certain amount of this exists but I have not included it in the foregoing list because it is not as widespread as the bulk of ordinary rhyming slang. It is recorded here for interest's sake.

Alabammy Sammy

Chanty Po Joe

Clydebank an Kilbooie Shooey, i.e. Hugh

Erskine Ferry, Finnieston Ferry, Govan Ferry Merry, a local pronunciation of Mary

Esso Blue Hugh

Peas an Barley Charlie

Puff Candy Andy

Scapa Flow Joe

Sparkin Plug Shug, i.e. Hugh

Steak an Kidney Sidney

Scrappies' rhyming slang

Again this is in limited use. My excuse for including it is that the few examples I have had drawn to my attention are both inventive and amusing. I am sure that similar specialist rhyming slang that I have yet to come across exists in other trades.

Denniston Palais Alley (short for aluminium)

Midnight Mass Brass

Missin Link Zinc

Pottit Heid Leid, i.e. lead

Phrases and Sayings

a blind man running for a bus wouldn't notice
Said jocularly of something that is considered good enough to pass a cursory inspection, having imperfections slight enough to make little real difference.

Ah could eat a farmer's arse through a hedge
Ah could eat a scabby dug
Ah could eat a scabby-heidit wean
All of these are meant to convey a level of hunger that compels one to abandon social taboos against such as cannibalism as well as allow no difficulty to deter one in getting at the food.

Ah could sleep on the edge ae a razor
I am utterly exhausted, asleep on my feet.

Ah could sook the face right aff you
A fairly direct chat-up line; slightly more robust than 'give us a kiss.'

Ah don't know . . . the ticket's fell aff
A cheeky response on being asked belligerently what you are looking at by a person who believes you have been staring at him. The insult is in comparing the person to an item in a shop window or a museum exhibit.

Ah never boil ma cabbages twice
I have no intention of repeating myself.

Ah'll see ye when ye're better dressed
A jocular farewell.

Ah'm meltin away to a greasy spot
I'm far too hot or overworked.

Ah've lost merr runnin fur a bus

An expression used to contemptuously dismiss a paltry sum of
money.

Ah've seen merr meat on a butcher's pencil

A male crack at a slim female; the kind of thing shouted from
a building site at women unfortunate enough to be passing by.
Other variants of this are:

Ah've seen merr meat on a jockey's whip
Ah've seen merr meat on a well-chowed chicken bone.

Ah wish ye health tae wear it

A conventional remark addressed to anyone who has recently
obtained some new item of clothing.

Ah wouldny go oot wi um if he fartit ten-bob notes

He's not my type. Such a feat, which is not even impressive
enough to win the speaker's affections, became still more
unlikely with the introduction of decimal currency.

Ah wouldny pull it fur a pension

An obscene jibe from a female to a male.

all over the place like a cheap coat

Applied to anyone or anything that is seen in many different
places. Kenneth Wright of *The Herald* traces this phrase back to
the Jewish community of Partick, many of whom made a living
in tailoring.

am Ah right am Ah wrang?

A conversational interjection seeking the listener's agreement.
The question is purely rhetorical as no-one actually expects to
be told he is wrong: 'No way are that shower gauny win the
league – am Ah right am Ah wrang?' 'Ye're right, son.'

another clean shirt an that'll be me (you, him etc.)

A jocular statement made about the supposedly short life
expectancy of a person who is mildly ill, perhaps complaining
of a bad cough, and so on: 'How's that cold of yours?' 'Ach,
another clean shirt an that'll be me.' Some people substitute
simmit for shirt.

a run round the table and a kick at the cat

If a harassed adult is preparing a meal and is continually pestered by children asking 'what's for my tea (or dinner etc.)?' he or she might reply with this phrase, which means 'nothing at all'.

as deep and dirty as the Clyde
Said about a person considered unscrupulous, devious, or secretive.

as high as a kite
Over-excited, unable to calm down: 'We couldny get the weans tae bed on Christmas Eve cause they were as high as kites.'

as Irish as the pigs of Docherty
Unmistakably a product of the Emerald Isle: 'Imagine him thinkin ma Mammy was a Tally, an her as Irish as the pigs a Docherty.' Just why Docherty's swine became a yardstick of Irishness I am at a loss to say.

as much use as a wet Woodbine
Of very little use whatsoever. Woodbine is, of course, a proprietary brand of cigarette.

as slow as a wee lassie
Applied to anyone considered dilatory.

as sure as guns (is iron)
Definitely: 'If ye don't get up this minute ye'll miss yer lift, as sure as guns.'

aw the nice!
An exclamation of pleasure at seeing something cute or sweet: 'Here's wan of her in her first communion dress ...' 'Aw the nice!'

better biled than fried
Said disparagingly of a scrawny person, usually by a male of a female: 'Ah'm no inty the skinny wan ... she'd be better biled than fried.'

better grey hair than nae hair
A greying person's riposte to being teased about silver threads among the gold.

bite someone's ear
　　To ask a favour of someone, especially to obtain something for nothing: 'See that jiner you know? Could ye bite his ear for a bit a plywood?'

bother your shirt (*or* **arse, backside, bunnit,** *or* **puff**)
　　What lazy or shiftless people do not do, i.e. make an effort, give a damn: 'Ye could have made a start while ye were waitin for me but ye didny bother yer shirt, did ye?'

breath like a burst lavvy
　　A withering description of the exhalations of a halitosis sufferer or of someone merely exhibiting one of the antisocial side-effects of a hangover.

by the way
　　This little phrase is notorious for turning up in every conceivable context, whether it belongs there or not. Like the similar tack-on expression **an at**, it has become a mere verbal space-filler or oral lubricant helping actual relevant words to issue in a reasonably fluid manner: 'See that bag a messages, by the way? Gauny root through it an see if there's any a they thingmies an at in it.'

can't see green cheese
　　Said about anyone who seems to want a thing simply because someone else has it: 'She'll no be happy till she's got a T-shirt the same as his. That wean canny see green cheese.'

come in if your feet's clean
　　A jocularly irreverent invitation to enter someone's home or office etc.

couldny hear him behind a caur ticket
　　A disparaging remark describing anyone who is either very small in stature or so quiet as to be insignificant. A caur, of course, is not a motor car but a tramcar, something not seen on the streets of Glasgow for over thirty years, yet this phrase came to my attention via a secondary school pupil. This is a good example of how useful or memorably vivid expressions

persist beyond the existence of the concrete things that gave rise to them.

couldny run a menage

A menage (pronounced *menodge*) is a savings club in a place of work. To say that someone is incapable of being in charge of such a thing is to accuse him of utter incompetence: 'Ah don't know how that wee clown got tae be a foreman ... he couldny run a menage.'

There are a couple of other similar phrases: **couldny run a flag up a pole; couldny run a two-door shithoose.**

couldny tackle a fish supper

Said of a footballer whose challenges are seen to lack bite, or more generally of anyone considered feeble.

could start a fight in an empty house *or* room

Said of someone who is naturally belligerent or loves an argument for its own sake: 'It wisny ma Robert's fault. That boay a yours could start a fight in an empty hoose.'

daft as a ha'penny watch

Applied to anyone considered silly or eccentric.

did ye faw an break yer watch?

An ironic, ostensibly sympathetic, enquiry to a child who has fallen and, although obviously unhurt, is making a fuss.

doesn't know if it's New Year or New York

Said of anyone who is obviously not thinking clearly, whether because of being none too clever to begin with, or feeling the effects of an intoxicant or a shock of some kind: 'Ah wouldny bother phonin him at this time in the mornin. Even if ye get him up he willny know if it's New Year or New York.'

dogs always smell their own dirt first

Said to someone who complains of a bad smell, particularly if he is insinuating that a person in the company is responsible for it.

don't give us it

Don't expect me to believe that: 'Look, ye were seen winchin in the bus shelter, so don't give us it ye wereny oot last night.'

don't give us yer worries
Stop complaining or moaning: 'Ah wish ye would just dae what ye're telt an no gie us yer worries.'
Similar requests include: **don't give us the beef; don't give us the bully.**

do you think my head buttons up the back?
Do you take me for an idiot? The image is of a dummy or scarecrow, anything with a head that is empty or stuffed with padding.

frighten the French
Something that a striking or fearsome woman (and it does always seem to be a woman) is said to be able to do: 'Allow her! She'd frighten the French, that yin.' The assumption that the French are particularly brave is, I suppose, a product of the Auld Alliance.

get stuck in like two men an a wee fella
To eat heartily; often an invitation to do just that.

gie's peace
Stop bothering or irritating me: 'Will you two gie's peace wi that shoutin an bawlin?'

go a place
A polite way of saying go to the toilet: 'Wait a wee minute. Ah just need tae go a place.'

go off like a two-bob rocket
To lose one's temper very easily and spectacularly: 'All Ah says wis "How's yer love life?" an he goes aff lik a two-bob rocket!' The image is of a cheap firework that, once lit, shoots straight up into the sky very quickly and briefly before fizzling out.

hair like straw hangin oot a midden
Said about any coiffure that looks untidy or unwashed: 'She goes aboot in the best a gear an her hair's like straw hangin oot a midden.'
A similar phrase is **hair like a burst couch**, comparing the crowning glory to the stuffing hanging out of a hole in a couch.

has emdy got a stick tae hit us wi?

An ironic rhetorical question posed by someone who is being verbally chastised and wishes to make the point that enough is enough.

have you been singin?

A jocular question asked of anyone who is carrying such a lot of small change that he is suspected of busking in the street or in back courts: 'Look at aw the smash he's giein us. Have ye been singin, or have ye done the meter?'

he gets his shoes made at John Brown's

Said of anyone with unusually large feet, implying that it takes a shipyard to construct his footwear.

hell mend you (him, her etc.)

Said to or about a person whose behaviour is likely to land him in trouble but who will not heed any warnings. I suppose the literal meaning is that if the person will not learn sense here and now he will repent at his leisure at the Bad Fire: 'Ye haveny listened tae a word Ah've said, have ye? Well, hell mend ye!'

he would drink it through a shitey cloot

A phrase applied to anyone so desperate for strong drink that circumstances which would deter the merely thirsty appear to present no obstacle to him. Other similar expressions include: **he would drink it oot an aul shoe; he would sook it aff a sore leg.**

hing aboot like a bad smell

To loiter around idly in a manner irritating to others: 'Gauny go oot fur a walk or somethin instead a hingin aboot the hoose lik a bad smell?'

hing aboot like a wet washin

To behave in a depressed or listless manner. This captures graphically the image of a person physically drooping like wet clothes on a washing line.

honey from the dunny

As a dunny is a basement or cellar in a tenement building, this expression is a label stigmatizing any woman who has come from a rough background and who, although she may try to maintain a veneer of sophistication, constantly gives herself away: 'The manageress stays in Newton Mearns but Ah know a honey fae the dunny when Ah see wan.'

hunger or a burst
Describes any state of affairs that is characterised by sudden swings from a period of relative idleness or scarcity to a spell of manic busyness or oversupply: 'Ah wish Ah wis in a steady job instead a this hunger or a burst carry-on bein self-employed.'

if Ah don't see ye aboot Ah'll see ye a sanny
A parting witticism, playing on *aboot* as *a boot*, a *sanny* being a sandshoe. There is also a suggestion of the use of *see* to mean pass or give.

if Ah don't see ye through the week Ah'll see ye through the windy
Another parting witticism; very funny the first time you hear it.

if at first you don't succeed, in wi the boot an then the heid
In this cheery message to anyone encountering difficulties, the traditional 'try, try again' has been replaced by something altogether more to local taste.

if he was chocolate he would eat himself
A disapproving assessment of someone who has a high opinion of his own worth.

if it's for ye it'll no go by ye
A fatalistic catchphrase meaning that what will be will be, that the events of life are somehow predestined and cannot be avoided by personal initiative. It tends to be used when something unfortunate occurs or is anticipated.

it aw goes the wan way
Said with regard to different types of food being consumed, indecorously, at the same time: 'Ah pulled um up aboot stickin a Mars Bar on a roll an aw he says was "It aw goes the wan way".'

it's nae loss what a freen gets

A conventional remark made by anyone who has given something to a friend, modestly deflecting any praise offered for the act of generosity.

it wasn't the cough that carried him off, but the coffin they carried him off in

A jocular catchphrase uttered when someone has a bad cough, not really meaning anything beyond a play on words.

it would bring a tear to a glass eye

Literally meaning that something is so moving that no-one can resist weeping, this phrase is more often used ironically to dismiss a claim for sympathy.

it would put a beard on ye *or* it would put years on ye

Said of something that is tedious or long and drawn-out. Each is an eminently down-to-earth way of putting over the idea that time seems to elongate when you are bored and you are made to feel as if a much longer period has elapsed than the real time taken: 'Goany turn it tae STV? It wid put a beard on ye, you an yer snooker.'

just swung doon oot a cherry tree

A phrase stigmatising someone as not worth listening to: 'Never mind what he says; that diddy just swung doon oot a cherry tree.'

kiltie kiltie cauld bum

An irreverent jibe chanted by children at any male in Highland dress.

let the bull see the coo

Said by someone who feels he has the necessary expertise for a given situation and wants any bystanders to move out of his way: 'Oot ma road yous. Let the bull see the coo till Ah get this sortit.' A similar phrase is **let the dug see the hare.**

like a fart in a trance

Applied to any distracted or listless person: 'Whit's the use a hingin aboot the hoose lik a fart in a trance? Away oot!' The relevance of *trance* is plain enough, but the concept of hypnotising anally-emitted gas is rather a surreal one.

like Sauchiehall Street

The name of one of the city's busiest thoroughfares is often applied to any bustling or crowded place: 'I'll come back and see ye when it's quiet ... it's like Sauchiehall Street in here just now.'

like two plums in a wet paper bag

An appreciative description made by a male as he views an attractive female posterior. A variation on this which is perhaps not quite so praiseful is **like two puppies fighting under a blanket.**

looks like he drapt a bad E

A fairly recent phrase, literally he looks as if he has swallowed an impure ecstasy tablet. It is used of anyone who looks either nauseous or in a dwam: 'Is that the new manager sittin ower there? Whit's his problem? He looks like he drapt a bad E.'

looks like he's ready for a clap with a spade

A rather callous remark made about someone who has the appearance of not being long for this world, having one foot in the grave, and so on.

Madras in evening, mad arse in morning

A smart little play on words, usually delivered as a 'wise old saying', intended as a salutary warning against eating a curry that is hotter than you can handle.

must have been a lie

The standard retort to anyone who says he has forgotten what he was going to say.

my name is Gough and I am off

A remark made by someone who is about to depart, its poetry almost qualifying it as rhyming slang.

never died a winter yet

A farewell remark at the end of a conversation about life's difficulties, meaning that the person concerned has up to now always come through whatever tribulations have arisen.

no for havin it

Not in favour of something; not willing to put up with it: 'Ah fancy tryin Turkey this summer but she's no fur havin it.'

nose running like a burn

A graphic description of one of the symptoms of a streaming head cold: 'That's me oot a paper hankies an ma nose is runnin like a burn!'

not a pick on

Used in describing a person considered over-thin: 'How in the name a the wee man does she need tae loss weight? There no a pick on her!' *Pick* in this sense (rather cannibalistically) means a morsel of food.

not enough to put in the corner of your eye

A very small amount indeed: 'Look at the wee bit a birthday cake they gannets have left for me . . . no enough tae pit in the coarner a yer eye!'

price of fish

Taken as a marker for inflation, this is frequently added to complaints for emphasis: 'What wi him an his sore back an the price a fish, it wid scunner ye.'

refuse nothing but blows

To accept anything and everything that is going, short of a gratuitous assault: 'Well, if ye're no wantin it gie it tae me. Ye know Ah refuse nothin but blows.'

say more than one's prayers

What an untrustworthy, and probably untruthful, person is said to do: 'Ah wouldny count on that happenin. She says merr than her prayers, that wan.'

smell of clay

When someone looks ill and may be considered as unlikely to live much longer, a rather ghoulish observer might make a remark along these lines: 'Did ye clock aul Morrison at the purvey? Wi the smell a clay aff him it's a waste a time him gaun hame.'

so dae Ah, sodie watter

A contemptuous remark made to a person whose sole contribution to a conversation consists of merely saying 'so dae Ah (so do I)' to any other individual's statements.

sufferin duck!

An exclamation, not meaning anything in particular, of exasperation, surprise, disbelief etc. Variations on this include **sufferin Americans** and **sufferin turkeys.** Why any of the above-mentioned should be perceived as suffering more than the rest of creation I cannot tell.

take the bad look off

To give a necessary improvement to the appearance of something: 'Ye'd think they wid gie their front door a wee lick a paint tae take the bad look aff it.' 'When Ah went in evrubdy wis up dancin except they two, sittin at a table full a drinks, an wee Boaby says "C'moan sit doon here an take the bad look aff us."'

that'll do me till Ah get somethin tae eat

A jocular remark made by someone who has just eaten a great deal and makes a joke of not being satisfied.

the band played believe it if you like

A remark expressing doubt about the truth of another statement.

the nights are fair drawin in

One of those conventional conversational remarks used more often as space-fillers than for their literal meaning, which in this case is that it is starting to get dark earlier these days.

the one the cobbler killed his wife with

A humorous label for the last of anything, e.g. the last drink of the night, the last teabag in a packet etc. The application is obvious when you consider what a cobbler is likely to use to murder his spouse: his *last*.

there's ma hand up tae God

An oath made to convince someone that you are telling the truth, often accompanied by physically holding up your right palm and placing the left, if free, over your heart. Often shortened to **hand tae God**: 'Ah'm tellin ye, hand tae God, no a word ae a lie.'

they're flyin low tonight
A code phrase, presumably dating from the war, used by one man to warn another that the zip of his fly is down.

thinks he's big but a wee coat fits him
A disparaging assessment of anyone who has an inflated opinion of himself, an example of a pronounced strain in Glasgow speech and attitudes: that of making sure everyone is cut down to size.

thinks he's honey and the bees don't know
Like the above, a remark made to pass comment on another person's self-esteem.

to a band playing
Indicates great willingness to take part in a particular activity: 'That wean a mines would eat grapefruit tae a band playin.'

toffs are careless
An observation made when someone is seen to be very generous or is spending a lot of money: 'D'ye hear what they rushed um fur that leather jaiket? Aye, it's well seen toffs are careless.'

The phrase is often used ironically when only insignificant sums are involved: 'Never mind the two pence change, son. Toffs are careless, ye know.'

up Suckie, doon Buckie an alang Argyle
A walking route through the city centre that has become a catchphrase: up Sauchiehall Street, down Buchanan Street, and along Argyle Street. When asked where they are going people often say this when they mean nowhere in particular.

up to high doh
Said of anyone who is overwrought or over-excited: 'The weans're always up to high doh on the last day of term.'

walk up and down till you're fed up

A remark intended to discourage someone from continually complaining about being hungry.

wan singer, wan song
Popularised by Billy Connolly, this catchphrase is supposedly shouted in a pub or club etc., when someone is trying to sing and others insist on joining in, to unharmonious effect. In everyday language it can also be heard as a call for order when there is a confused debate going on: 'Hey yous, wan singer, wan song, eh? Let the boay speak his piece.'

what's the crack?
A conventional remark, equivalent to 'what's happening?' or 'what's going on?' Also used to request information on a particular topic: 'What's the crack wi these new local authorities?'

whit d'ye want me tae dae . . . burst oot in fairy lights?
Said by someone refusing to be as excited or impressed as a person making some kind of announcement thinks he should be.

whit is it wi you?
A question, essentially meaning 'what makes you like this?', addressed to a person whose behaviour is annoying: 'Whit're ye moanin aboot noo? Whit is it wi you the day?'

why are we so good?
A chant sometimes heard at football matches when supporters are so happy about their team's performance that they find it hard to comprehend why they are so blessed.

wouldny be held nor tied
A descriptive phrase used about anyone who is extremely agitated, angry, or impatient: 'Ah wis late wi the wee soul's twelve o'clock feed. By the time she got her bottle she wouldny be held nor tied.'

wouldny be me
A stock assessment of a situation showing the speaker's disinclination to act similarly: 'Whit? Marry a guy that's got weans already? It wouldny be me, pal.'

wouldny gie ye

These words appear as the overture to quite a range of phrases stigmatising meanness. Here are a few examples:

he wouldny gie ye a fright on a dark night
he wouldny gie ye a spear if he wis a Zulu
he wouldny gie ye daylight in a dark corner
he wouldny gie ye the itch
he wouldny gie a blind sparra a worm

wouldny make a back for a waistcoat

Said of someone considered very small or puny: 'The size a him, tryin tae jine the polis! He widny make a back for a waistcoat.'

wouldny say eechie or ochie

Wouldn't say one thing or the other; wouldn't say yes or no.

wouldny walk the length of himself

A phrase used to condemn a lazy person: 'He's one of these guys that goes to the gym twice a week but wouldny walk the length of himself.'

would ye credit it?

Would you believe it? This is so much of a catch-phrase that it has been used, punning on the sense of *credit,* by companies advertising their easy-payment facilities.

yer jaws are gaun the right way

Literally, you are physically able to eat, this is used ironically by someone seeing another person eat heartily: 'Have another doughnut, wee yin. Ah'm that glad tae see yer jaws're gaun the right way.'

ye wouldny need tae be . . .

A number of phrases begin with these words which are equivalent to 'it's a good thing that you are not'. For example: 'Ye wouldny need tae be easy offended when ye hear the language ae um.' 'Ye wouldny need tae be in a hurry, the time ye've tae wait oan this bus.'

School Nicknames

The thing about these is that they are used cheerfully (or otherwise) by both staff and pupils alike. The following list represents only those I have come across; I'm sure there are many more out there.

The Bella Bellahouston Academy

Hutchie Hutcheson's Grammar School

The Johnnie St John Bosco

The Maggie May St Margaret Mary's Secondary

The Mungo *or* **Muggo** St Mungo's Academy

The Queenie Queen's Park Secondary

The Rock St Roch's Secondary

St Disgustin's St Augustine's Secondary

The Wally Dishes St Aloysius College

Some of Yer Auld Patter

Many readers of *The Patter* and *The Patter – Another Blast* have written to me suggesting items of vocabulary that I chose not to include because they were not only too old-fashioned but often referred to things that no longer existed. While it is still my aim to document *current* Glasgow language, I feel it would be a shame to let some of these words and phrases be lost without record. For this reason I offer below a selection, by no means a comprehensive list, of older Glaswegianisms, many of which, as may be seen, spring from recollections of childhood.

as two-faced as the Briggait clock Very hypocritical.

Barney Dillon Rhyming slang for *shillin*, i.e. shilling.

bundy A time-clock, as formerly used on tramcar services to record journey times etc.

caur A tramcar, often found in the plural **the caurs**: 'She got a job as a clippie on the caurs.'

clabber dance An informal dance held in a tenement back court (where participants would have to dance on *clabber*, i.e. dirt or mud). Apparently people would hang carpets and sheets over washing lines to screen out wind and give the illusion of being indoors.

dollar Five shillings. **Half a dollar** was two shillings and six-pence, or a half-crown.

doolander A wide flat bunnit, or man's cap; broad enough for a doo to land on.

figure To be **in one's figure** is to be lightly dressed, with bare arms etc., as on a warm day: 'Ah see ye're in yer figure today, Mr Liston.'

Hairy-Leggit Irishmen A nickname for the HLI (Highland Light Infantry).

half a toosh A half-crown.

Hi Hi, the A nickname for Third Lanark F. C., a former well-supported Glasgow side, based at Cathkin Park. Also known as **the Thirds**.

hunch-cuddy-hunch A game played by boys, involving climbing onto one another's backs.

KDRF A mischievous children's game, explained by the full form of its initial letters: Kick Door Run Fast.

kick the can A children's game, involving elements of hide-and-seek, in which the seeker must also prevent his prey from sneaking out to kick an agreed object, usually a tin can.

moshie A game played with marbles.

ring-bell-skoosh Similar to **KDRF,** a game involving ringing a doorbell and then running away.

tartan banner Rhyming slang for a *tanner,* i.e. a sixpenny piece.

thrummer A threepenny bit.

Tobermory tottie A sweetie, consisting of a chewy disc, dusted in cinnamon powder, in which would be concealed a small plastic toy. A confection hazardous to the teeth in more ways than one.

winkle A penny (pre-decimal).